WHY ARE WE CREATED?

WHY ARE WE CREATED?

INCREASING OUR UNDERSTANDING OF HUMANITY'S PURPOSE ON EARTH

Sir John Templeton

and

Rebekah Alezander Dunlap

TEMPLETON FOUNDATION PRESS

PHILADELPHIA AND LONDON

Templeton Foundation Press
Five Radnor Corporate Center, Suite 120
100 Matsonford Road
Radnor, Pennsylvania 19087
www.templetonpress.org

Designed and typeset by Gopa & Ted2, Inc
Printed by McNaughton & Gunn

Library of Congress Cataloging-in-Publication Data

Templeton, John, 1912-
  Why are we created? : increasing our understanding of humanity's
purpose on earth / by Sir John M. Templeton and Rebekah Dunlap.
    p. cm.
Includes bibliographical references (p.133).
  ISBN 1-932031-29-4 (pbk.)
  1. Spiritual life. I. Dunlap, Rebekah Alezander. II. Title.
  BL624 .T43 2003
  291.4'4—dc21   2002153741

Printed in the United States of America

03 04 05 06 07   10 9 8 7 6 5 4 3 2 1

Contents

Introduction

TWENTY-FIVE CENTURIES AGO, Xenophanes, and twelve centuries ago, Shankara, taught that possibly nothing exists independently of God, and that God is immeasurably greater than all of time and space, let alone the visible earth and its billions of inhabitants! In the twentieth century, modern sciences have come to realize how very tiny the earth is when compared with the billions of galaxies or even when compared to our own Milky Way galaxy. We also realize how brief human history is in comparison with the age of the cosmos. Yet, *here we are!* And although humans may seem to be the most sophisticated species presently on our planet, perhaps we should not think of our place as being at the end of cosmogenesis.

This book was written to raise a number of thought-provoking questions regarding the age-old challenge and quest for increasing understanding of humanity's purpose on Earth; in other words, to ask: "Why are we created?" One of our intents is to encourage thoughtfulness, observation, and research for *multitudes of evidences* of purpose in this tantalizing search that has intrigued humans for so long. We hope to point to evidence that may indicate "purpose" for humanity has been a beneficial force in various fields of human activity in areas such as health, education, character development, the professions, science, physics, cosmology, and religion.

Perhaps asking pertinent questions regarding humanity's purposes that stimulate pondering and research by people of various ages and diverse cultures can help humans gain greater enthusiasm for further wide-ranging and open-minded research. *Why Are We Created?* appears to be a subject that almost everyone has thought about at some time during his or her travels along this journey of life. The evolving process of human life on Earth seems abundant with innovations and superb timing. Can human lives become more productive and beneficial if we discover additional ways to become helpers in divine purposes?

We also preface this book with an awareness that the Creator of this awesome and wonderful universe is presently beyond our human capacity to measure or understand. If ancient people could usually imagine God as a spirit separate from what may now be considered "reality," are we egotistical to think that God can be in any way smaller or more limited than total reality?

Consider this historical fact for a moment: We knew less than one billionth of the cosmos before the research of Nicolas Copernicus. And look at the tremendous advancements for humanity that his discoveries have brought about! Søren Kierkegaard taught that the human race advances on the backs of those rare geniuses who venture into unexplored realms where many fear to tread. Only in the past few decades have we come to appreciate the enormity of the cosmos and the paucity of our knowledge of it. However, when we consider the rapidly expanding reservoir of human knowledge, is it possible that within the next two centuries human perception of realities can be multiplied over one hundredfold?

We know so little of divinity. Yet, it seems that this Creator is also the God who would be known! What evidences substantiate this perspective? Let's look at a statement from the book *The God Who Would Be Known*:

> Our thesis is that God is revealing himself in his immensity at an ever-accelerating pace through rapid developments in the sciences. The sphere of the spirit is expanding exponentially all across the scientific landscape. Among the most prominent features are the fields of cosmogony — study of the origin of the universe — and of molecular biology. In between these two extremes of the galactic and the molecular stand two other prominent areas of rapid development: the studies of universal order and human evolution.[1]

Does increasing evidence indicate that invisible realities may be vastly more basic than things visible? Can research reveal that the spiritual could be the foundation of the material life? It would appear that human exploration of our universal Creator is just beginning and can become both an intriguing and humanly beneficial voyage into the realm of the spirit.

The more we know about the universe and our place in it, the more we realize how little we know. One of the benefits of examining the vast development of the created cosmos is that by doing so, we may obtain a sufficiently broad perspective to begin to discern purposes or plans — perhaps even an ultimate meaning — in the evolutionary process. Great minds are beginning to see the reality that lies behind fleeting appearances and pertinent questions are being raised and researched.

EXPANDING AND EVOLVING

Have you heard the expression that life on Earth serves as a school for the soul? Various major world religions have described Earth as a school. Perhaps we could give this idea some consideration. Using the school analogy, if Earth can serve as a school, does each life become a classroom for experiential exercises? Is part of our "homework" learning ways to expand our consciousness and grow spiritually? How do spiritual maturity and strength grow? Can spiritual growth take place through a variety of avenues? For example, might growth occur through the application of human reason and research? Can openness to divine revelation represent an avenue of growth? Surely, the diligent use of the various talents given to each of us provides learning opportunities.

Is our universe an orderly system whose nature is to evolve? In some respects, a lifetime on Earth may seem a slow way to educate a soul. And fifteen billion years may seem a slow way to erect the school building! However, to put things into perspective, could divinity have created what we also call "time"? What is the purpose of time? Is its role to make room for learning, for growth, and for developing our ability to give love?

OPPORTUNITIES TO LEARN

If Earth *is* a school for infinite purpose, wouldn't a likely question be: Who are the teachers? Life is often filled with joy and sadness, challenges and overcoming, successes and difficulties—all of which offer opportunities for learning and progress. Can we perceive how these ranges of thoughts and feelings, situations and experiences play a constructive teaching role in our lives? From a divine perspective, would our soul's education be incomplete without these experiences?

WHAT IS THE ESSENCE OF OUR PURPOSE IN LIFE?

Might a purpose of infinite intellect be to express itself in increasing varieties of lesser intellects? Is it possible that we may be here to become servants of creation or even helpers in divine creativity? Were human beings created to be agents of God's accelerating creativity? Can humans discover larger fractions of infinite intellect? Could we be the beginning of a new evolution as the first creatures in the history of life on Earth to participate consciously in the ongoing creative process? Are we rewarded when we strive to increase our own intellect or to give our children better intellectual opportunities? How can we discover and more effectively utilize our gifts and talents? Who are we? Why are we created?

In *World Scriptures: A Comparative Anthology of Sacred Texts*, the human being is described as "a microcosm of the universe, having the essences of all things in himself or herself. As the microcosm, human beings have the foundation to know, use, and enjoy all things. Of all creatures, humans have the widest scope of thought and action, encompassing all things, knowing and appreciating all things, guiding and prospering all things, and transcending all things."[2] The Talmud tells us: "All that the Holy One created in the world He created in man" (Abot de Rabbi Nathan 31). The Qur'an states: "Do you not see that God has subjected to your use all things in the heavens and on earth, and has made His bounties flow to you in exceeding measure, both seen and unseen?" (31.30). In the Hindu Srimad Bhagavatam 11.2, we are told: "Truly do I exist in all beings, but I am most manifest in man. The human heart is my favorite dwelling place." Christian Scripture begins the story of Homo sapiens with the words "Let us make man in our own image, in our likeness" (Genesis 1:27), then later asks the questions:

> What is man, that thou art mindful of him?
>   And the son of man, that thou visitest him?
> For thou hast made him a little lower than the angels,
>   And hast crowned him with glory and honor.
> Thou madest him to have dominion over the works of thy hands;
>   Thou hast put all things under his feet:
> All sheep and oxen, yea, and the beasts of the field;
>   The fowl of the air, and the fish of the sea,
> And whatsoever passeth through the paths of the seas.
>
> O LORD, our Lord, how excellent is thy name in all the earth!
>
> (Psalms 8:4–9)

Provocative spiritual concepts such as these help extend our desire to encourage further individual research. They may also stimulate a new personal perspective regarding the age-old question of human purpose. Perhaps we can present a selection of helpful materials to encourage deep-seated human research and raise exciting questions focusing on some of the following possibilities:

+ What is the importance of recognizing the presence of the sacred within us and around us?

✦ Out of our desire to change the world for the better, could
  we learn that the principle of creation is change and that
  through change God's creations will continue and accelerate?

✦ Is a possible purpose for our being to help accelerate God's
  creativity, similar in some tiny ways to how humans recently
  created intelligent computers?

✦ What evidence indicates that the invisible can be over one
  hundred times larger and more varied than the visible?

✦ How can individuals create a purposeful and fruitful way
  of life?

✦ Are the happiest people those who are most productive in
  their life's journey and those who bring much happiness to
  others? How does happiness relate to one's purpose or vice
  versa?

✦ How can the humble approach to life help us experience
  our purpose and express true and lasting joy?

Many philosophical and theological writings suggest that our purpose here is to move from lower levels of living to higher and higher
planes of expression. Sometimes, we may seem to stumble in our life's
journey. Yet, those "stumbling blocks" can actually serve as stepping
stones, helping us to acquire and generate the necessary energy to propel ourselves to the next level of consciousness and creativity. Every
experience is an opportunity for growth.

UNIVERSAL LAWS AND SPIRITUAL PRINCIPLES

We often speak of the laws of nature as a useful analogy or comparison. The law of gravity expresses the nature of the gravitational interaction between bodies like a planet and its sun. Our Earth and our sun are one example. Are these patterns of behavior the outcome of the basic nature of creation of which we are a part? We recognize that there are laws of nature that appear to be expressions of the character or being of physical objects in creation. Is it also reasonable to expect there may be analogous laws of the spirit that are expressions of the character of spiritual realities? These laws of the spirit refer to patterns of voluntary *human* behavior, not to the involuntary behavior of physical objects. Does our world operate on spiritual principles or laws just as it operates on the natural laws of physics like the law of gravity? Universal laws affect all phases of a person's life. Their unique characteristic seems to be that they are always effective, whether or not we believe in them, or even whether or not we are aware of them! A person is free to choose to learn about these laws and act in accordance with them. Could part of our development through the physical plane be to gain a greater awareness and understanding of these principles and utilize the knowledge in our lives for beneficial purposes?

POSSIBILITIES FOR SPIRITUAL PROGRESS

Why Are We Created? was written with the express desire of helping you, the reader, unfold a more useful and happier life. As we begin to understand more of our purpose as finite creatures in a vast universe of infinite complexity and intricacy, perhaps our growing awareness of universal principles can help us release restricting prejudices. As we put into daily practice our increasing spiritual insights, opportunities occur for us to open our minds and hearts to greater awareness of, and beneficial participation in, the great plan of which we are all a part. The ability to choose to move to a higher spiritual level of consciousness and to a happier, more fulfilling way of life lies entirely within each individual. A universal divine intelligence flows through all of us. As we begin to elevate the thoughts, feelings, and actions of daily decision making in our individual lives, surely we will be making progress on the path of the sacred quest for all of humanity.

There is a wonderful universe within each of us — a unified field of abundant possibilities. Consider exploring the questions asked and the ideas offered in this book with your family, friends, and associates. How can you further research these possibilities and enlarge your understanding? An open door for further education is an invitation to live and learn! Share your thoughts. Ask questions. Respond from your present and personal perspectives to the questions raised in the various chapters of the book. Deepen your relationship with the concepts presented. Explore ways to activate some of these ideas in your everyday life. What new ideas and perspectives can you contribute?

Take your time with this book. Assimilate its words, ideas, possibilities, and messages into your mind, heart, and soul. In doing so, may you understand more of why you were created and move into a joyously adventurous, beneficial, and purposeful way of living. May you find a sense of direction that can bring together the needs of the world with your unique gifts. And may you know that . . . God loves you, and I do, too!

John Marks Templeton

PART I

WHY ARE WE CREATED?

CHAPTER I

The Splendor That Can Shine!

Is God all of you and are you a tiny part of God?
—JOHN MARKS TEMPLETON

HAVE YOU EVER STOOD on the seashore, looked out across what seemed to be an infinite expanse of ocean, and contemplated what wondrous achievements bordered the opposite shore? The creative imagination might visualize progressive cities bustling with people of every description who are involved in a wide spectrum of adventures. Did you also perhaps wonder what mysteries might be embraced as part of the vast sea rolling between where you stood and that far distant shore?

Humanity is presently poised on another kind of shore—the shore of expanding exploration, new discoveries, and accelerating knowledge. We stand on an impressive foundation of research and evidence and concepts secured over the latest five centuries of accelerating scientific progress. Our vantage point rises like a high cliff. Before us lies an immense, uncertain ocean of reality from which future knowledge will be obtained. How large is this ocean? Where could its exploration take those who will live in the future? The vista is tremendous, exciting, and humbling in its vastness!

With an attitude of open-minded exploration of possibilities to develop our minds and our spiritual capacities, can we learn more about the Creator's purposes for us? Might we find, as in the words of Scripture, "Things beyond our seeing, things beyond our hearing, things beyond our imagining, all prepared by God for those who love him?" (1 Corinthians 2:9–12). Is this the spirit we have received from the Creator that allows us to move and sense and participate in the rich reality that surrounds us? Is this spirit part of the hidden splendor of every human being, luminous as the stars? Is this spirit the splendor that shines through every person as a unique expression of divinity?

A SUCCESSION OF WONDERMENT

Thinking about this omniscient Creator raises numerous questions: Is our human consciousness only a tiny manifestation of a vast creative consciousness that is often referred to by a variety of names such as God, Allah, Spirit, Yahweh, Brahman, or the Creator? Has our human concept of this creative source been too small? Is our concept too centered on our human species? What is our relationship with this infinite divinity? We exist. We think. We feel. We play. We work. We aspire. Toward what ultimate purpose do we aspire? What evidences indicate that the invisible can be over one hundred times larger and more varied than the visible? When considering the fruitfulness of the notion of creation, do we see that possibly a most important aspect of the divine purpose can be realized through ongoing creativity, change, and innovation? How can we learn ways to embrace progress and discovery in a manner that taps the deep symphonies of divine creativity and evolves us in life's purpose?

Ancient humans sought answers to such questions. Present day men and women often find themselves returning to these ancient musings. And future generations will most likely continue and speed up the search. It seems the quest to find answers to such ultimate questions may be rooted in the very deepest parts of the human soul. What might we learn if we applied the same intensity of research energy to the pursuit of spiritual information that has been devoted to scientific inquiry? The world is presently in a state of unprecedented technical expertise, yet our knowledge of our own spirituality has not progressed at the same pace.

From remarkable signals of transcendence that have been placed in the heavens, on Earth, and within ourselves, some conclude that this universe is here by divine plan. We have looked at the origin of the universe through various sciences, explored sacred teachings from different world religions, studied the evolution of humans, and found varieties of evidences of infinite divinity. Is it now time to channel our creative restlessness toward building a world in which exploration and progress is vigorous in spiritual aspects of life as well as in scientific, technological, and economic ones?

Is there a cosmic design for humanity that imbues our consciousness with holiness and prompts us to wonder whether we are tiny parts of divinity? Does this same universal design expand human imagination with the beauty of infinite creative expression, open our hearts to the unlimited love of God, and invite our diligence to align with infinite creative intention? Is it now time to explore avenues for greater understanding of the question: Why are we created?

How dramatically would our spiritual knowledge increase if we enthusiastically became more receptive to the endless possibilities that await us in our spiritual lives? What could happen in each person's individual life, and for humanity as a whole, if we began to place more focus on the infinity and magnificence of Spirit and on our relationship with the creative source of everything? How would our world progress if we made strong commitments to scientific exploration of our mental and physical expressions of life as humans?

WHAT ARE WE?

Before considering humanity's place in universal reality, it might be helpful to look at what we are as individuals. We are bodies that can see and touch. We have minds that think thoughts and we feel emotions. We are souls that sense truth, beauty, goodness, and love and are part of an inner Spirit that so devotedly leads us forward. At the core of these aspects of being human lies the human will, serving as the ship's captain of personality, choosing, deciding, acting, and determining our life's course.

Our souls long for relationship with God—by whatever name we call the Creator of all there is. We long to know this Creator in magnificent expressions of love, life, creativity, peace, beauty, compassion, companionship, and more. Could we possibly be longing for something that is hidden within? Are we already imbued with divine power to progress toward the goals we desire? Is life an adventure to develop our innate divinity? Could this be part of the reason why we are created? Does the urge to live creatively come from inner prompting of the divine imagination that pushes itself into expression through us, as creative ideas? Is this part of the magnificent creative research that can shine through our thoughts, feelings, words, deeds, and the way we live our lives?

We live, knowingly or unknowingly, under spiritual principles, universal laws of life that can reflect the energy of the Creator moving through each person. Perhaps remaining reflective, innovative, and balanced—while doing our best every day—helps us make significant progress toward noble goals. The divine idea for our lives seems so

much greater than we may have previously imagined. Often new channels of exploration open for greater expression and fruitfulness. We
begin to establish an actual way of living, with a growing awareness of
possible participation with the creative source.

SOME PERTINENT COMMENTS
ABOUT PURPOSE

Daniel H. Osmond writes:

> Purpose has to do with ends, "That for the sake of which a thing
> (person) exists." One can ask the purpose of the universe, or of
> the world, of animate beings generally, or of humans specifically.
> And, in relation to humans, several levels of purpose can be iden-
> tified, ranging from the basic requirements for physical survival
> and gratification to the ultimate and most searching intellectual
> and spiritual issues of life. Sooner or later, thoughtful people ask,
> "For what sake (purpose) do I exist?" They do so when crises con-
> front them, if at no other time, but, of course, the purpose of
> one's life should no more be contemplated only in times of crisis,
> than the purpose of one's automobile should be pondered only in
> times of traffic accidents. . . . Purpose can range in scope from a
> primal fight for survival to the highest levels of intellectual and
> spiritual aspiration and attainment. . . . It is worth discovering
> "true purpose" for the whole of our lives, if such a thing exists.[1]

As human beings . . . We are about to jump off the cliff. We may
have free will, but at this point in our evolution we do not have
free choice. We will either jump off the cliff into a life lived by

faith in ourselves just as we are, or we will be pushed off the cliff [by life]. One way or the other, as the Scripture says, "We shall not all sleep, but we shall all be changed" [1 Corinthians 15:51].

To jump off a cliff means to let go of all the mental and physical things or people that we have been holding on to. We have to let go of all our old concepts, all our pet theories, all our mind stuff, as well as those co-dependent personal relationships we are anchored to. In order for us to move into a conscious realization that two parallel worlds exist—the world of spiritual beingness and the world of material sense—we have to jump off the cliff! That doesn't mean we won't continue to have the loved ones and loved things we currently cherish, but we will have to let go of dependence on them.[2]

The most fascinating phase of the human journey is its spiritual development. . . . Humanity's fascination with a spiritual dimension, a hidden sphere of power, an underlying ordering principle that lies unseen behind everyday events as well as gigantic happenings, has grown and taken on new importance in the ensuing centuries. . . [E]ach new explanation seems to open up deeper questions, as though we still see only the outline of things and explain our observations by means of models that only approximate the truth. . . . [T]he sphere of the spirit will spread and energize new creative dimensions of understanding for future humankind.[3]

[W]e live in a spiritual world and every individual in that world has been created in God's image with unique gifts and a purpose to use those gifts to contribute value to the world.

Purpose is already within us. It is there waiting to be discovered. If we open ourselves up to what's inside us, we'll discover it. And once we discover it, we will have to try to live it. . . . Working on purpose gives us a sense of direction. . . .Purpose is a way of life — a discipline to be practiced day in and day out. . . . Spirit touches and moves through our lives through the mystery of purpose.[4]

LIVING IN A THREE-DIMENSIONAL WORLD

Could there be many of us who have not, at some point, heard the inner whisper, "There is more to life than what you may be presently experiencing"? And we began to search for that hidden splendor of Spirit that wants to shine forth. With a focus on the infinity and the magnificence of divinity and on our relationship with this creative source, we can begin to explore more deeply our spiritual and physical expressions as humans.

Were human beings created to be agents of God's accelerating creativity? Our human ability to create and to understand appears vastly greater than that of any other kind of earthly creature. Various religious texts point out the possibility that even a beclouded mind may be intrinsically pure and contain the germ of divinity. Analects 7.29 in Confucianism states: "Is goodness indeed so far away? If we really wanted Goodness, we should find that it was at our very side." God is described in the Qur'an as "nearer than the jugular vein," knowing all a person's thoughts and desires, and abiding within the human heart. Sufis interpret the Qur'anic parable of the lamp as expressing the presence of God in the human heart as a light, illuminating the lamp of the body. In Hinduism, Sikhism, and Jainism, the divine immanence is described ontologically: Ultimate reality is the self.

Yet, living in a three-dimensional world, we continue to find examples of our limited ability to describe our Creator and our relationship with divinity. The following story from our book, *Wisdom from World Religions: Pathways Toward Heaven on Earth*, provides a possible example of this relationship.

ARE YOU THE CREATOR'S APPLE TREE?

A young man named John inherited a fertile and productive farm that boasted a large apple orchard located at the back of the property. This orchard was proclaimed throughout the area for producing the best tasting and juiciest apples. In the fall, when apple-picking time arrived, people traveled to the farm from miles around to pick and purchase the apples. John welcomed everyone who came to buy apples and there was always an abundance of the fruit.

John had a special connection with the orchard. He remembered, as a boy, following his father among the apple trees as he cared for the orchard. When John was ten, his father gave him a pot containing a planted apple seed. The tiny seed grew into a tender young tree that John planted in the ground. He watched the awesome miracle of his special tree growing from the tiny seed, eventually into a beautiful tree, billowing with blossoms that became delicious fruit. John learned a lot about apple trees. He learned how the tree lifted water from its roots up through the trunk and into its beautiful, fragrant blossoms. He watched bees swarm around the blossoms, gathering nectar to make honey. As years passed and John grew into adulthood, he watched the apple trees survive storms and sub-zero hardships to again blossom in the spring and produce more tasty fruit in the fall.

One day, while sitting beneath his special tree, John experienced an awakening. He realized he knew a lot about his apple tree and could easily describe its attributes. But the tree's perceptive abilities were not expansive enough to comprehend its gardener! There, with the warm sun caressing his shoulders, a gentle wind ruffling his hair, and the tree supporting his back, John realized he knew as little about his own Creator as the apple tree did about him!

Why should we expect to be able to describe our Creator when we know so little about divinity? Probably no person has yet learned even one percent of what humans can learn about divinity. For example, in only two centuries, has science research discovered over one hundredfold more information previously invisible and inconceivable about cosmology, subatomic realities, electronics, and cellular activity? Examples of accelerating discoveries may be found in results from research in various areas such as medicine, agriculture, and electromagnetism. Can even more awesome discoveries be made about such basic spiritual realities as unlimited love, purpose, intellect, creativity, and prayer?

Are you the Creator's apple tree? Evidence indicates that we are created through infinite love and truly flourish when we radiate unlimited, overflowing love for our Creator and for every other human being — without exception.

We are the recipients of so many divine blessings. We always have the opportunity to draw from the reservoir of spiritual substance as much as we may choose to receive and use. When we begin to realize and appreciate the wonders of creation, we grow in beneficial ways. We can reflect the essence of the apple tree in our story: beautiful, fragrant, vital, productive, filled with purpose, and beneficial to many.

THE ORDERING PRINCIPLE

Are deep and powerful ordering forces a part of our universe? If universal law or principle is inherent in the Creator's purpose for all creation, is there a perfection with which all creatures exist according to the laws established for and in them? Does one of the strongest hints for understanding the creativity of the cosmos relate to its capacity for so-called self-organization? Current science leads us to observe a universe seemingly filled with creativity in the direction of cooperative and organizational processes. How did these processes come about? Could one of the strongest evidences for the ordering principle be that most wondrous phenomenon called human self-consciousness? Are we merely at the "beginning of the story" in discovering our attributes of self-awareness and self-conscious purpose? How can human beings cooperate with the existence of this transcendent reality to a greater degree?

Some have considered the ordering principle to be the first law of the universe. Indeed, could there be any universe unless its parts were maintained in complex order? The facts of Spirit are of spiritual character and, when understood in their right relation, are they orderly? Is orderliness, as a universal principle, the test of true science? Is there also a divine idea of order or adjustment that is established in man's thought so our minds and affairs can cooperate with universal purpose?

Is order an evidence of purpose? Does the extraordinarily complex origin of life argue for a marvelous creativity, connection, and order? The process seems to seethe with innovations and a superb timing that dispels any notion of blind chance. Is this process a part of increasing our awareness of our immortality and our multidimensional being?

Does a higher consciousness guide us all from our inner and outer space? Have the scientific voyages into outer space invariably directed us back to researching our inner space? For many, the fantastic view of the planet Earth from space symbolized a unique birth of consciousness. As those early astronauts gazed down upon our brilliantly colored sphere in the black depths of space, they were transformed.

ENCOURAGING CREATIVITY
AND PROGRESS IN OUR LIVES

How can our growing spiritual research encourage creativity and progress in our lives? When we live as Earth-plane beings, drawing primarily upon our human faculties, we present to the world and to each other a selfhood of human qualities and human awareness. This human self may seem limited, finite, and consisting mostly of what we have learned through education, personal experiences, environment, and other exterior influences. Hidden behind this personal self, however, abides the reality of our being. We are much more than the physical and mental person. We have a spiritual identity and the physical and mental are included within the spiritual.

Could our relation to the Creator be like that of a sunbeam to the sun? Nothing can separate the sun from one of its rays. Made of the sun's substance, partaking of its nature, each sunbeam has a particular mission, a certain spot to caress and warm and light. Like the sunbeam, we, too, have our own special spot to fill. We have our own special work to do. Thus, we are part of the divine plan and necessary to the perfection and health of the whole. Could divinity's plan for us be so great that we have only glimpsed it occasionally, but are those glimpses the light that leads us through the seeming darkness of ignorance to greater discovery?

Think about this idea. Can you imagine anything more meaningful or more powerful than realizing your true purpose—and then stepping forward to attain it? Because of our oneness with Spirit, creative power is our power. Every day we use that power in hundreds of ways, sometimes constructively and sometimes destructively.

THE CREATIVE POWER OF IMAGINATION

Have you considered that at every waking moment we are imagining or using our imaginations to express this universal creative power? Every time we interpret and activate the images that come into our minds, we affect our own lives and our world in some way.

How can we effectively and beneficially utilize this wonderful faculty of imagination? Through ideas and concepts! Concepts have been called imagination's fuel. When we repeat a desirable concept often enough, it can eventually become an automatic part of our consciousness. One example is reading inspiring books and focusing on spiritual principles. When we focus on this avenue of research, study, and awareness, we eventually create an affirmative groove of mental receptors and connectors. We can visualize new possibilities and bring them into manifestation through creative planning.

PRINCIPLES AND CONCEPTS

Let's look for a moment at the possible connection between spiritual principles and human concepts. Concepts are objective. They can take on form. The dictionary says that a concept is something that is conceived in the mind, and that to perceive comes from a Latin root word, "percipere," meaning "to take hold of." What we "take hold of" or perceive can become a very real and productive concept in our personal awareness. So, does it follow that how we *perceive* reality actually plays a powerful role in how we actually *create* our reality?

How does perception tie in with spiritual principles? One of the great universal principles is often called the Law of Mind Action. Expressed another way, "Thoughts held in mind produce after their kind." Or, "As you think, so you are!" Thus, it would seem that a concept would not exist apart from how the mind perceives it and how spiritual energy animates it. With this in mind, could there be any thing or any action that does not represent the presence of, or the movement of, Spirit or creative energy?

Reflecting on the question "Why are we created?" can help expand our framework for inquiry into greater spiritual dimensions of discovery regarding humanity's purpose. Often, "purpose" implies looking to the future. We might ask: What are we going to do next to get where we want to go? From a conscious human perspective, the future may seem uncertain and the attainment of our goals may be a matter of conjecture. Does the creative source have the infinite wisdom to draw on in this completely spontaneous dream of life to aid the tiny human in the Earth dimension? Indeed, is one purpose of our lives to be a vehicle for the Creator to enhance the whole expanse of human expression and emotions?

A New Era of Progress

The Creator promises to reveal himself to those who seek. May we hope to discover a little more about humankind's relation to its Creator by exercising humility appropriate to the subject of our inquiry? Open-minded questioning and research help enlarge discovery of the unknown and keep the door open to further investigation and progress. Is it possible that the Earth and its inhabitants may be entering a new era of spiritual progress more exciting and beneficial than anything yet experienced? As mentioned earlier, the development of humans on Earth may not be the end of creation, but the beginning of it!

Many have taught that those who worship the creative Source are empowered by the Spirit and spiritual exploration and that growth can be a means of being lifted to new heights of joy, love, and philanthropic achievement. The divine Spirit moves into our lives and makes us over from within so that all things are seen in a new light. Unlimited love often becomes a spontaneous expression of a spirit-filled soul.

In his book, *My Philosophy and My Religion*, Ralph Waldo Trine put it this way:

> Great spiritual truths — truths of the real life are the same in all ages, and will come to any man or any woman who will make the conditions whereby they can come. God speaks wherever he finds a humble listening ear, whether it be Jew or Gentile, Hindu or Parsee, American or East Indian, Christian or Bushman. It is the realm of the inner life that we should wisely give more attention to. The springs of life are all from within. We must make the right mental condition, and we must couple it with faith and expectancy. We should also give sufficient time in the quiet, that we may clearly hear and rightly interpret.[5]

Should not each of us work for self-improvement through seeking to understand to a greater degree why we are created? If the Earth is a great classroom when considered from an eternal point of view, would not one of the important lessons to learn while on Earth — that of building a radiant, loving, successful, fruitful life — be up to us?

Emanuel Swedenborg wrote that we will not be in heaven until heaven is in us. If building our heaven is up to us, why should we waste even one precious day? Right where we are at this moment, we can begin to acknowledge the life and spirit of heaven within us. We can accept the challenge to express life to its fullest potential.

REFLECTIONS ON LIFE

What are some ways you can research some of the concepts presented in this chapter?

✦ Is the visible only a tiny, temporary manifestation of reality?

✦ What do you aspire to achieve during your lifetime?

✦ What does the word "reality" mean to you?

✦ What are your thoughts and feelings about the idea of the "ordering concept"?

✦ Are you enthusiastic about discovering more about the Creator?

✦ What would it mean to you and to your life to learn more about why you were created?

✦ Do you want to support researchers using scientific methods to discover more about ultimate reality?

CHAPTER 2

The Power of Purpose

Spirit touches and moves our lives through the mystery of purpose.
—RICHARD J. LEIDER, THE POWER OF PURPOSE

EVER SINCE MANKIND began to think about its past and sought to understand the threads of progress, many theories have evolved regarding human origins. Even in this "enlightened" age, the early stages in the onward course of human development are often approached through a shadowy twilight that precipitates more diligent researching. Have you ever considered exploring this question: Why is the human spirit incarnate in a physical body? Could the purpose of human existence on Earth be a combination of spiritual, intellectual, cultural, and physical evolution?

The spiritual aspect of man has been compared to a seed. Like the apple tree mentioned in chapter one, the vibrant seed puts forth its young shoots, stems, leaves, and eventually grows into full flowering. As the mature plant is inherent within the seed, is the immortal germ of the Creator inherent within the human soul? What evidence is there that the Creator lives in you and you in the Creator? Are many human potentialities present from birth? Does life as experienced in a three-dimensional world offer vast opportunities to express these potentialities?

For the silently developing seed, is not every experience valuable?

Are human beings, like seeds, strengthened by the winds of adversity, purified and refined by the rain of sorrow, enhanced by nurturing experiences, elevated by noble purpose, and beautified and expanded by the sunshine of love and happiness? Are dynamic and fruitful abilities and capacities continually opening to greater expression in the form of the developing human soul? Does a growing inner strength emerge that often precedes great possibilities?

Our five senses provide us with the capacity to perceive only a few of the myriad notes in the complex creative symphony of life that surrounds us. The unknown extends vastly beyond the area of the known. Can the restless and searching spirit of humanity attune our minds to perceive greater evidence of creation and expressive creativity? Has the Creator given us free will for new interpretation of eternal truths so that in our limited way we can be creative?

THE INCREDIBLE HUMAN

"What a piece of work is man!" exclaimed Hamlet. Indeed, humans are, in the words of the psalmist, "fearfully and wonderfully made." Through his studies of the miracle of the human body, the late well-known biologist Alexis Carrel became deeply aware of the complex inner structures of energy and power that work with cosmic wisdom in and through the physical human expression. He perceived this network of energy and power as forming an intricate part of the true and enduring man. Carrel saw a timeless yet largely unknown and unrecognized creation, and found an auspicious area for exciting additional exploration! Is the time now ripe to consider further ways and possibilities in which humanity is a tiny manifestation of this astonishing cosmos? Is the individual self possibly a temporary manifestation of the pattern of a much greater and vaster reality? How would our per-sonal lives be affected if we considered that the physical body could be a dynamic spiritual expression rather than a strictly material one?

The composition of our physical body constantly changes in an ongoing process. What about our conscious mind? Are we continually searching, researching, learning, and growing through mental open-ness and agility? Over the journey of a human lifetime, any unfolding day can offer a plethora of possibilities. We might experience ups and downs, successes and failures, profits and losses, and situations we may term "good" or "bad." These seem to be part of the Earth-school expe-rience. How are we utilizing the wisdom we gain from these experi-ences?

THE CALL TO THE HEIGHTS

Changes occurred slowly in prehistoric times. The primitive mind began a gradual search for knowledge and understanding of the pur-poses for the existence of human beings. Cave paintings, engravings, and tool manufacture changed with progress. A more logical plan of life became an increasing necessity. Perhaps a personal philosophy began to develop from individual experiences and was applied to the processes and problems of living. These changes could have been sparked by the life drama ceaselessly occurring within and around each person. However gradually, life experiences affected thoughts, feel-ings, and individual behaviors.

Then, perhaps the divine nature inherent in all humans began to whisper, "There's more!" Could it have been an inner invitation from universal creative energy? Did it stimulate individuals to aspire to greater heights of spiritual exploration? Could this compelling inner urge be one reason why the "call to greater spiritual heights" seems to be of immense importance to vast numbers of humans? Many of us experience an innate desire for meaning, direction, and purpose.

A new avenue of inquiry, thought, research, and study opens before the questing soul. An almost passionate longing for deeper wisdom and the opportunity to apply it to life may be experienced. Does the call of our spiritual destiny often manifest as the deep drives and natural talents that help form our personalities? Is there another element vitally important to this "heart call"? If life progression is to be effective, fruitful, and enduring, must a purposeful philosophy of life be adopted?

HEARING AND RESPONDING TO THE CALL

Our capacity to hear the inward call and respond to it seems to be steadily increasing. Visions and goals once perceived as ideals may now constitute a compelling necessity. The inner call often helps shape our chosen area of work, improves our relationships, and advances the quality and direction of our lives. Is this how the outstretched arms of Spirit lift the aspirant to greater awareness—helping us to transform our attitudes, the way we live, how we view our health, and every other facet of our lives? What changes begin to occur in character as we respond to these noble purposes?

Following our purpose may require us to reach more deeply to tap our inner resources. Making the decision to rise to greater personal and spiritual heights often requires commitment, courage, open-mindedness, and focused effort. If we have prepared for life's adventure by recognizing and overcoming challenges, improving our weaknesses, and expressing gratitude for our blessings, our journey may be less difficult. We begin with present circumstances and move forward. Everything that has previously transpired in our lives brings us to a point of opportunity. And although countless ages have come and gone, man is still searching and asking the question: Why am I here; why was I created?

If you had the ability to explore possible responses and arrange your life in a more fruitful progression (and the opportunity does exist!), would you consider it fruitful and beneficial to exert strong effort toward achieving this goal? Would you be willing to direct your conscious thoughts toward linking with the creative energy of the universe? Are you ready to explore a unique and vast realm of possibilities? If so, let's go!

OUR LINK WITH UNIVERSAL ENERGY

Are there strong indications of ultimate realities beyond what humans have yet discovered? Does one of these indications relate to our understanding of the creativity of the cosmos and its capacity for self-organization? There appears to be a continuity of organization into novel and increasingly complex structures and relationships throughout the spectrum of transitions from stardust to thinking man and beyond. How do these changes come about? What processes are involved? How can we more effectively utilize our growing awareness of the astonishing cosmic order that the sciences repeatedly reveal? How are humans a manifestation of this astonishing cosmos? Is our material world a possible incubator, provided by the Creator, in which human spirits can develop and seek ultimate expression in a realm invisible to us? How can studies of man's purpose contribute to the greater reality around us?

Can a study of interesting phenomena—life and humankind—lead us to evidences of our link with universal energy? How can we unravel more of the mystery of possibly the most highly endowed organization of matter that has yet been researched by science? Continued questions? More research? Johannes Kepler, one of the most creative astronomers of all time, believed that the heavens declare the glory of God. In his article "Dare a Scientist Believe in Design?" Owen Gingerich wrote: "Kepler's life and works provide central evidence that an individual can be both a creative scientist and a believer in divine design in this universe, and that indeed the very motivation for the scientific research can stem from a desire to trace God's handiwork."[1]

DISCERNING OUR PURPOSE

How can we discern the purpose of our being created in ways that are consistent with what we know of the universe through the sciences? Through history? Through theology? Through world religions? Could the realization that we live in a cosmos endowed with fundamental order, transparent to our understanding and characterized by profound rational beauty, indicate a creative source and purpose behind the flux of the world's becoming? Is the fact that the human mind has the capacity to "unlock the secrets of nature" an evidence of our link with the creative source? When our consciousness is directed outwardly, it seems that the manifested world takes precedence. When our consciousness is directed inwardly, can we then research our own source and form a link with universal creativity? Can we form a bridge between the invisible and the manifest worlds?

Is realization or enlightenment a condition in which the sense of self progresses from a limited material awareness to one that is infinite and formless? The wave cannot measure the ocean, yet there is a vital point of contact between them. In like manner, is there a point of contact where infinite divinity connects with the finite? Is this a possible avenue through which we may discover more of how the Creator expresses divine consciousness into the multitudinous finite forms of life and the various universes life may inhabit?

Creation seems to include the esthetics of intelligence and the emergence of life into endless displays of beauty and grace. From our present awareness, the human being is considered possibly the most intricate of the Creator's creations. Although we are made of Earth elements, the power and complexity of divine consciousness present in the body may be beyond our current human conception. Within and behind those physical cells of the body flow the electrical currents of life. And behind those subtle energies are our thoughts and perceptions. As we further develop the spiritual aspects of our being, a shift in consciousness often takes place and we increasingly begin to realize our kinship with all of life. Thus, are we both the product and the witness of Creation as a continuous and eternal process?

To enjoy the loveliness of a fragrant blossom may be pleasant. To comprehend the reality beyond the blossom provides an opportunity to behold an aspect of the face of the Creator. Enjoying the rhythm and harmony of wondrous music is uplifting. Yet, can this experience compare with the magnificence of hearing the voice of the Creator immanent in the finite beauties of creation? Can living in the consciousness of divine spirit be another powerful link with universal creative energy? Have we already been given everything we need to work toward a productive and beneficial life? Is part of our task to recognize our talents, assemble the tools, and use them productively?

POSSIBILITIES FOR SPIRITUAL GROWTH

When we awaken in the morning, we rise from the depths of sleep to awareness of our surroundings. We may glance at the clock to determine the time of day and read the newspaper to learn of current events. As we dress and prepare to move into the day's activities, we may have a momentary awareness of our individual presence. In a short period, we recapitulate an adventure that has taken millions of years: the awakening from the depths of unconsciousness!

In *What We May Be,* Piero Ferrucci wrote: "It is precisely this awareness of self that makes it possible for us to experience solitude and love, to be responsible to other human beings, to be aware of the past and of the future, of life and death, to have values, to be able to plan ahead, to be conscious of our evolution and perhaps to be able to influence its course."[2] With this awareness, what is our next step? What are some possibilities for spiritual growth that can move us closer toward understanding the power of purpose and finding our personal purpose in life? How may we make the best use of, and benefit from, our present situation? How may we most productively express our creative energy?

KEEP AN OPEN MIND

One of the initial steps is very important. *Keep an open mind and develop a spectrum of spiritual consciousness.* What does this admonition mean? Spiritual consciousness is a vast subject indeed. Consciousness has been compared to a sword that may cut through a leaf and become stained by the sap of the leaf, yet the sword itself is not changed. As the majestic river that courses through the valley comes from a source, so can the "river of consciousness" flow from the source of the consciousness of the Creator that is beyond all creation.

DEVELOP A SPIRITUAL CONSCIOUSNESS

Developing a spiritual consciousness can occur by directing our thinking processes in positive ways to achieve greater good and to produce attunement with the creative source. The trend of human thought and consciousness may change. Thus, maintaining an unbiased, open, and unprejudiced point of view can be a major step forward in growth. And remember, just because others may think differently from the way you think does not necessarily mean that either is "right" or "wrong." Listen. Learn. Let go of your ego for a moment. Our greatest enemy is often ourselves! Hold to a firm mental resolve to be the most beneficial and productive person you can be!

DISCOVER THE GIFT OF INNER SPIRIT

Discover the gift of spirit within you. Use it to strengthen your spiritual muscles. Put these muscles to work for you. Spiritual faculties can be awakened and developed to a greater extent than you can imagine. A spiritually-oriented consciousness embraces a wide field of activity. It has the capacity, in its expression, to influence many individual minds and, therefore, events. Could a continuation of the function of science be a study of consciousness itself? Would this be a fruitful area for investigation to further human evolution? To be a spiritual person does not mean to be an angel with wings but to be something much greater —a soul in touch with infinite divinity!

One of the simplest ways to begin to spiritualize your consciousness may be through the activity of prayer. When prayer plays an important part in our daily lives, we often make better decisions and become more productive in beneficial ways. We may also become increasingly introspective. Understanding and forgiveness may come more easily to us. We may be less resentful. It is easier for someone who prays to be a friend.

Each of us enters the Earth-life experience with a great storehouse of spiritual treasures, some of which may lie just beyond our present conscious awareness. Can these spiritual attributes be enhanced by diligent research, thus leading to an accelerated spiritual development of all of humankind? Can you perceive how enhancing our spiritual gifts may contribute in moving all of us toward our purpose?

FINDING JOY

Finding joy in life can prompt spiritual growth. This special joy is continually rhythmically changing while its core remains unchanged. It is anchored in divine purpose! This joy can scintillate through us like shimmering stars in the sky! Joy is like a garden of flowering qualities. Do the qualities of unlimited love, joy, peace, compassion, and noble purpose that can grow in the garden of human hearts merely reflect the beauty and glory of the Creator? Is the spirit of joy so powerful because it is multifaceted? Joy can provide assurance. It can serve as a healing agent. Joy is reciprocal. The joy we express is often felt and shared by others and returns to us in abundance. Joy easily lies within our power to express because no person, condition, circumstance, or outer influence can really separate us from the energy of joy or prevent us from sharing it with others.

WHY IS HAVING PURPOSE
SO IMPORTANT TO PROGRESSION?

What would our lives be like if we confidently and continually released the divine creativity within us? One primary purpose for human life seems to be to create a life that is as fruitful as possible. This may constitute living in such a way that we feel good about ourselves and what we accomplish. Purpose may guide us to act in such a manner that the good we accomplish lives on and reflects our noble calling. Is having a purpose in life a contributing factor toward increased productivity? Does perceiving our purpose help us establish a definite direction for focusing our energies? Having a targeted purpose often encourages preparing a guideline for accomplishment and for affirmation of a set of values.

HIGH AIMS AND CLEAR PURPOSE

High aims and clear purpose can act as rudders, steering the unlimited and unique potential of our minds toward beneficial productivity. Purpose empowers our thoughts, feelings, and actions toward greater accomplishment. Interesting possibilities may be explored in the quest toward a specific goal, providing valuable knowledge and experience. Then, when we find opportunities in line with our talents and goals, we may feel better prepared to seize the moment.

To live successfully in the outer world, it seems equally important to live successfully in the inner world. As within, so without. Have you ever considered the invisible part of you and how it contributes to your overall purpose? When you look in a mirror, you see an image of yourself. Every day we are visible as physical bodies. But what about the ways we manifest our fundamental invisibility?

Try an experiment for a moment. Gently close your eyes. Your body is now invisible to your sight. How do you know you exist? Do you feel your body's weight? If you are seated, do you feel the chair that is supporting you? What are the sounds you hear? What smells are you aware of? In this moment, you are "real" in terms of your senses. Now, open your eyes. Are you the physical form you can see, or are you that inner being you were conscious of when your eyes were closed? In the greater reality, you are both a visible and an invisible magnificent nucleus of energy around which many thoughts are revolving. Can you recognize the importance of cultivating an understanding and developing a conscious working relationship with both the inner and outer aspects of your being?

WHY IS HAVING PURPOSE IN YOUR LIFE SO POWERFUL?

An old adage says that the ridden horse runs faster because a rider on the horse can use the reins to guide the horse in a more precise direction. Making a decision about what you want to achieve can be similar to putting a bit into a horse's mouth. The bit is probably the smallest part of the harness of a horse, yet it is the most important. When the bit is in place, the movements of the horse can be guided. With a gentle tug on the bit, we can direct the horse to move his body in whatever direction we wish it to go. Without guidance, the horse may run wild or go off to munch grass in the pasture!

Without a vision or a goal to inspire us and stimulate us to greater expression, we may not achieve the useful and progressive lives we desire. If we do not have a plan or know what we want to achieve, we may fail to achieve much! Unlimited opportunities prevail to utilize our thinking ability in constructive ways as we go about our daily tasks.

Setting Goals

How does establishing goals provide us with opportunities to develop greater potential? Practice is usually essential for mastering something new. The more we practice a skill, utilize a talent, or work with a chosen vocation, the more proficient we become. Obstacles can become steps to growth. We may learn to praise the unexpected events that shatter our preconceived idea of how things "should" be. Our minds may be sharpened through new insights. Our focus can become clearer. Greater self-determination and assurance and a stronger emergence of willpower can occur. We may approach a truer recognition and appreciation of our strengths. Fear is often diminished. Our imaginations become enriched. There may be an awakening of our intuition. These possibilities represent some of the ways that having purpose may be powerfully reflected in our lives. What are some other "potential developers"?

Life is filled with transition and change. A person may feel a strong impulse or inner call to move in a new direction. Ask yourself: If I am being "called" to loftier heights or to follow a different path, who is doing the calling? Could this inner urging be an expression of Spirit at work? Every step along the path is both a singular experience and a part of the whole of life. Can purpose change with the circumstances of life? Is it possible that as we move toward a specific purpose in one direction, we may suddenly find that a different choice would fulfill our purpose in a more beneficial way? Could this realization make purpose an ongoing discovery? Following your purpose means using your gifts and abilities in ways that deeply move you.

The Power of Purpose and the Power of the Present

If we closely examine our minds and thoughts, we may get a sense of the possibility that only the now moment exists. We can remember the past, but it only exists in the present memory moment. We may anticipate the future, but it, too, only exists in the present memory moment.

How many of us have said, "Mañana, I will do it tomorrow"? Often an initial response to this expression is to set aside the object of consideration until another day. But wisdom tells us to never put off until tomorrow what we can accomplish today. Tomorrow will bring its own unique challenges and opportunities. Our response is often more effective if we are not carrying the weight of yesterday's "leftovers."

The more we allow ourselves to focus on events, whether past or future, the more we miss the most precious now moment. Why is the present moment so precious? Primarily because that's all there is! Is it possible for anything to happen or to be outside of the present moment? Consider this idea: What we think of as happening in the past actually happened in a now moment. What we may anticipate as happening in the future will also happen in a now moment. What we think of as the past is a memory that was stored in the mind as a former now moment! We cannot bring back one millisecond of past time or move a fraction of a second into the future. We can only live in the present moment. Moment by moment!

Our minds are superb tools when used appropriately. The present moment can hold a powerful key to liberation. What could happen if we chose to be fully present in the now moment? Would we leave our analytical minds and their falsely created egos behind and move into a significantly higher altitude of spiritual awareness? Could an amazing transformational experience occur when we become willing to be fully present in the moment and feel the reality of expressions like prayer, unconditional love, thanksgiving, compassion, steadfastness, humility, and a beautiful mind? Would ordinary living become an extraordinary experiencing of the present moment?

Are there really any ordinary moments in life? This moment—right now—is full within itself and not something separate from our lives. It is a part of the whole. It is rich with potential and possibilities. So how can we create a purposeful and fruitful way of life *now?* How can we access the power of the now moment? Perhaps a good beginning would be to focus on the practical realm of day-to-day living and step out of the time dimension as much as possible.

Train yourself to be present as the silent watcher of your mind. Be observantly aware of your thoughts and emotions and responses to various situations that may occur. How often does your attention drift to the past or anticipate the future? In *The Power of Now,* Eckhart Tolle tells us:

> Identification with the mind creates more time; observation of the mind opens up the dimension of the timeless. . . . Once you can feel what it means to be present, it becomes much easier to choose to step out of the time dimension whenever time is not needed for practical purposes and move more deeply into the Now. This does not impair your ability to use time—past or future—when you need to refer to it for practical matters. Nor does it impair your ability to use your mind. In fact, it enhances it.[3]

We live in a magnificent time of transition. We are living in an age when human information has multiplied over one hundredfold in less than a single century. We are experiencing a time when research in consciousness is rapidly gaining momentum. We can utilize this time wisely.

TODAY!

Today is the most important day of your life. Today's steps are the ones we need to take. Today's challenges are the ones we need to meet. Today's decisions are the ones necessary to make. Tomorrow is the next episode in a great adventure and it will come, heralding its own good. But the present is here now. Today we can live to the fullest expression of our being. Today we can exert our best effort. Today we can laugh in the sunshine of creation. Today we can savor the sights, sounds, and opportunities of life. Today we can diligently apply all lessons the past has taught us to living in the now. Today offers a divine connection between the power of human purpose and the power of the present moment. Today is our opportunity to serve, to love, to understand, and to grow in cosmic consciousness. Let us use the moments of this day with wisdom. Then, when this day is finished, we can lay it gratefully aside and give thanks to the Creator for today's unique experiences, for there will never be another day exactly like this one!

REFLECTIONS ON LIFE

✦ Could part of our purpose be to live so radiantly and creatively that our personal world might quiver with excitement and enthusiasm and bring forth a new spirit of possibility?

◆ Are we here, in part, that life may discover, know, and express itself more abundantly through us for the blessing and fulfillment of all of creation — past, present, and potential?

◆ How has our understanding of our world and our place in the universe changed in recent decades through the momentous discoveries of science?

◆ What do you hope to achieve in your lifetime? What role does creative energy play in your goals?

◆ How do your personal beliefs affect the way you are presently living your life?

CHAPTER 3

Opening Wide the Door to Opportunity

Enthusiasm facilitates achievement.

—JOHN MARKS TEMPLETON

HOW WOULD YOU RESPOND to this question: What do you desire beyond all else? Many people might answer, "A good life!" A longing may be expressed to experience beauty and the highest emotions, or to possess boundless energy to meet daily responsibilities. We may choose to live on a higher level of physical strength, mental interest, noble purpose, and spiritual meaning. For some, "living a good life" could be based on a value system that includes joy, enthusiasm, gratitude, purpose, and spiritual perspective.

How does Spirit touch and move our lives through the mystery of purpose? We live in a spiritual as well as in a physical world. The elusive answer may not necessarily be found in the realm of the known or be readily apparent in our present personal experiences. Rather, an increased understanding of Spirit and purpose might be discovered in what we have yet to accomplish and from further research in the realm of the unknown. Materially, the unknown can seem to be a huge void. Potentially, the unknown can be the reservoir for many discoveries. And research into unknown areas can represent a tremendous doorway to opportunity.

RECOGNIZING OPPORTUNITIES

Opportunities abound for the soul that is alert and awake, diligent, and open to giving and receiving. How often do we take advantage of the opportunities that life brings to our attention? And what is an opportunity? Could an opportunity represent heaven's call for us to acknowledge and fulfill our highest destiny? Could an opportunity also be an occasion to explore our unique essence that is sometimes called the divine spark within?

Barbara Brennan wrote:

This spark has no beginning and no end. It cannot be measured in terms of time or space. It is both individual and universal. It is like one light that shines within everything, and yet maintains a distinctive essence within each of us. When we are fully aware of this unique inner radiance, we feel what it is to be utterly alive. We experience unconditional love. We sense complete safety because that spark also connects us to the universal divinity within all things. We feel that all life, within ourselves and others, is precious. We respect, delight in and affirm one another's differences. The more we affirm one another in this way, the more we are capable of greatness. [1]

In the past few decades, the sciences have opened our awareness to a universe so vast and complex that our view of humanity, of our world, and of our Creator would seem to require a searching reassessment. How can we objectively look at ourselves and at the conditions in our lives? How may we more beneficially and successfully integrate our lives with the world around us? How can we begin to release negative habits and replace them with positive possibilities? Is intelligent and informed change in our view of life one of the keys to progress?

Humanity's search for meaning has long been a primary life motivation. Each person has the freedom to embark on the discovery of this meaning. Evidence indicates that the search for meaning and purpose has been a beneficial force in areas such as physics, cosmology, medicine, and human character development. Most people recognize a need for purpose and meaning in their lives. Many desire to make a viable contribution to something that is important to them. For example, consider that teenage suicide is almost unknown among young people who have found a noble purpose. Why do you think that may be?

GROWING IN AWARENESS

How awake are you? G. I. Gurdieff said, "Man is asleep."[2] How can we become more "awake"? How often, in our ordinary state of consciousness, do we stay in direct contact with what is actually happening around us? And *thinking* about being fully present is not the same as actually *being* fully present! What benefits can we experience from being more mindful, alert, and aware? Cultivating an attitude of being mindful on a daily basis can help us perceive with greater clarity, accuracy, and discrimination what is taking place. How can we direct our thoughts for more beneficial action?

What we may describe as our reality seems to be constantly changing and understanding subtle shades of differences in situations is often necessary. How can conditioned habits of thought, perception, feeling, and action be transformed into more vital, loving, beneficial, and intelligent ways of life? What could our lives be like if we made the commitment to continue to grow in awareness?

Sir Isaac Newton said, "I do not know what I may appear to the world; but to myself I seem to have been only like a boy playing on the seashore, and diverting myself in now and then finding a smoother pebble or a prettier shell than ordinary, whilst the great ocean of truth lay all undiscovered before me." And Freeman Dyson described his quest for purpose in the following way:

> Somewhere in that great ocean of truth, the answers to questions about life in the universe are hidden. . . beyond these questions are others that we cannot even ask, questions about the universe as it may be perceived in the future by minds whose thoughts and feelings are as inaccessible to us as our thoughts and feelings are to earthworms. The potentialities of life and intelligence in the universe go far beyond anything that humans can imagine. Theology should begin by recognizing the vastness of the ocean of truth and the pettiness of our search for smaller pebbles. [3]

BUILDING A HEAVEN ON EARTH

In our search to learn more about our purpose and why we exist, how may we make a stronger connection with the infinite mind and the unknown? Is our deep desire for knowledge a strong justification for our continuing quest? Are we here, in one respect, because embedded in our human nature may be a possible code for heaven's self-realization—here on earth? Is it possible that research in genetics can accelerate the progress of human intelligence? In fact, on one level, does all our scientific research in a variety of fields bring us further information about the nature and vastness of the Creator?

Can we realize more of heaven on earth through self-discovery and

self-understanding and by growing in wisdom through active participation in everyday living? Is consciously and deliberately evolving
toward a wiser and more luminous state of being part of human purpose? What are some ways we can assist this process? What kind of
future can develop from recognizing the possibility that we may be
partners, indeed, co-creators, with divinity?

A young person may ask the question: How much success can I
achieve in life? As he or she matures, the question may be: What is my
life really about and how can I make a difference? Are we more fully
alive and beneficially productive when we relate our lives to the lives
of others? How can our lives become increasingly fruitful and beneficial as we help others along the way?

Nearly two thousand years ago, a Talmud sage taught that the Cre-
ator could have created a plant that would grow loaves of bread.
Instead, wheat was created for us to mill and bake into bread. Why?
Could it be that we are partners in the continuing work of creation?

ACCEPTING AND CREATING OPPORTUNITIES

What attitudes and endeavors can help us accept the opportunities
that are before us? How can we create new opportunities to augment
our progress? Could spiritual research about invisible realities such as
love, purpose, creativity, intellect, thankfulness, prayer, humility,
praise, thrift, compassion, invention, truthfulness, worship, and a spirit
of giving provide beneficial knowledge and growth?

Enthusiasm is considered such an important quality because it often
spells the difference between mediocrity and accomplishment. How
can the seeds of enthusiasm be encouraged to grow? Practicing or

expressing enthusiasm helps it become a more effective attribute in life. And when practiced regularly, enthusiasm can open wide the door to unlimited opportunities! Ralph Waldo Emerson wrote, "Every great and commanding moment in the annals of the world is a triumph of enthusiasm." His powerful statement expresses a wondrous truth. It is difficult to stifle the ardor or dampen the spirit of someone who really believes in what they are doing—someone who is working with purpose!

How can we develop the habit of expressing hopeful and enthusiastic ideas? What endeavors could help us look at the positive side of every situation, experience, and person? What are some ways we can express greater gratitude for the life-producing and life-supporting powers that are present everywhere?

As previously mentioned, each of us may be on the Earth for a special purpose. Does it then become each person's responsibility to determine what he or she can do to help make the world a better place? And then take steps to go out and put our ideas to work? How about creating opportunities for ourselves so that our efforts become like tiny seeds planted in the garden of life? How can we:

- ✦ Live together with others beneficially, joyfully, and peacefully?

- ✦ Be more honest with ourselves and with others and live with integrity?

- ✦ Stand strong on principle without yielding to expediency?

- ✦ Sense the presence of something greater than we may presently comprehend?

- ✦ Find delight in the smallest and simplest things?

✦ Put into practice the maxim: "Give a man a fish and you feed him for a day; teach him how to fish and you feed him for a lifetime"?

✦ Take full responsibility for our actions?

✦ Continue to spread goodwill, regardless of appearances?

✦ Do our part in beneficial ways for future generations in a world that often appears to be going through rapid changes?

✦ Be resolute and unflinching in accomplishing the toughest tasks, knowing that no effort sincerely extended for good is in vain?

✦ Internalize the spiritual principles of noble qualities and continuous improvement at all levels of life?

✦ Experience as much of ourselves and our world as possible?

CULTIVATING A SPIRIT OF ADVENTURE

The things we believe and the habits we develop often condition what we think we can or cannot do. Our beliefs often become habits of thinking, feeling, and perceiving. We may sometimes allow our talents and abilities to be defined by old, worn-out, useless concepts that can be like restrictive stakes hammered into the ground. Therefore, in order to take a bold step toward new discoveries, it may be necessary to do some mental housecleaning.

Ask yourself some searching questions. How long has it been since you explored the basis for your beliefs? An important aspect of training your mind is learning to observe your beliefs in operation and becoming aware of the consequences each has for helping improve mankind. Then, the choice may be made to retain a belief, change it, or release it altogether. If you discover a belief or habit you would like to research, how would you go about doing so?

Do your characteristics include noble virtues such as strength, humility, altruism of spirit, honesty, compassion, gentleness, understanding, forgiveness, kindness, and perhaps the greatest of these, unlimited love? Do you fill your mind with thoughts that are positive and productive? Do you approach others with kindness and patience? Do you fully maximize the power of noble purpose? Successful people usually live their virtues consciously. If a person places a particular virtue — honesty, for example — at the top of his list of ethics, what benefit does it provide to him and to others?

Creative expressions often enhance our feelings of individuality and personal worth. How do you feel about your creative ability? How do you feel about your spirituality? When we are in touch with our spiritual natures, our conscious and subconscious minds become synchronized in appreciation of our essential worthiness. Can you perceive how asking some of these questions might cultivate a spirit of adventure that can lead to beneficial opportunities?

A spirit of adventure is not a philosophical teaching; rather, it can be a living standard for a noble and productive life. Evolution reflects the engagement of a situation, experiencing it, and emerging to the other side of the experience. Every life situation can be an evolving continuum, endowing the adventurer with a richness of experience and wisdom. The process often involves setting up standards of performance that help us evaluate the results. Usually, experience (more than mere words) increases knowledge. Living life fully may not result in finding answers, but the quest itself causes us to evolve!

EVALUATING PRIORITIES AND VALUES

Does part of the quest to understand our purpose involve evaluating our priorities and establishing a beneficial set of values and ethics? What expressions, situations, or changes might result from becoming simultaneously aware that we have an essential spiritual or invisible presence as well as a physical presence? Do our priorities shift as the invisible becomes as real or perhaps more real to us as than the visible and material realms? How does material advancement, along with the advancement of the physical sciences, coincide or balance with developing spiritual realization? How does the invisible power of divine consciousness become an experiential reality? Is the path of progress and the road to spiritual integration of the wholeness of body, mind, and spirit more positively paved by the principle of priority?

We may talk enthusiastically about our spiritual values and our goals in life. However, if our priorities are in an ineffective or non-beneficial order, can we accomplish what we desire? As we mature spiritually, how are we more influenced by Spirit's inner guidance? Is part of our goal to better understand our purpose and the holiness within and become living expressions of both? To live successfully in the outer world, is it equally important to live successfully in the inner world? How does one aspect compliment the other?

Yogananda wrote, "Only spiritual consciousness — realization of God's presence in one's self and in every other living being — can save the world."[4] And we must begin with self. How do our values help us live a more constructive life that can then reflect outward into our world? Is there something eminently practical and personal about expressing our deepest values, virtues, and noble purposes? Noble purpose creates fruitful lives.

What are some steps that may be helpful along the way toward fruitful and beneficial demonstrations of our life patterns? Are we demonstrating noble human qualities such as honesty, integrity, kindness, respect for others, unlimited love, self-discipline, wisdom, justice, and humility? Certainly, discipline and self-control contribute to our learning experience, but a life of purpose, enthusiasm, and creativity is certainly worth the effort. Living a life filled with purpose could be a doorway toward achieving lasting happiness.

UTILIZING GIFTS AND TALENTS

Imagine an underground spring, flowing in unseen depths, ready to burst forth in abundance, bringing nourishing waters for anyone who may be willing to dig deeper. How are you and your life similar to this vibrant underground spring? What unknown and untapped resources wait just beneath the surface of your conscious mind? How enthusiastic are you about discovering more of your gifts and talents and utilizing these precious attributes?

What we are is the Creator's gift to us. What we may become is our gift to the Creator. Our gifts and talents often grow proportionately with our commitment to use them for a higher purpose and greater good. The inner gifts of expression, sensitivity, and spiritual discernment can be ready resources in service for others.

Think about these gifts for a moment. *Expression* allows us to convey special words and feelings, enabling us to serve as an inspiration for others through our enthusiasm, strength, and support. *Sensitivity* can help dissolve conventional barriers between ourselves and others through subtle dimensions of perception and experience. We have an opportunity to empathize with others and to offer a loving capacity for understanding and support. *Spiritual discernment* can be a wonderful help in maintaining alignment with spiritual principles. Opportunities can be limitless when we seek to fill a need in humanity or to offer service to others. And the person who is willing to say *Yes* to experience is the person who often discovers new frontiers!

When considering how you may better utilize your gifts, talents, and abilities, think about the mirror principle. When you look in the mirror, you see the reflection of your own face. You smile and the face in the mirror smiles. You frown and the frown is reflected back to you. What is the message here? Could it be, "As we give, so shall we receive"? What we see in others and in the world is often a reflection of some aspect of our own being.

FROM "STUMBLING BLOCKS" TO "STEPPING STONES"

Oftentimes an occurrence that may seem to be filled with difficult elements of human necessity can prove to be an occasion for experiencing a tremendous "divine" opportunity! Wisdom encourages us to look for the lesson or gift any experience may bring. Sometimes what we may consider a "stumbling block" on life's journey may become a vital "stepping stone" to success in our endeavors. The difference is often found in how we meet the situation and in the choices we make.

Consider the truism that a problem cannot be solved on the same level as the problem. A successful problem solver is often someone who creates a new context from which to view the problem or situation. This may be accomplished by directing the focus of attention away from the distracting details of the difficulty. Then, from a detached perspective, we may be able to examine the available information and explore a variety of options. A beneficial course of action may then be chosen.

Sometimes, one of the most difficult obstacles to overcome is that of self. If we remember that we carry within our souls, our minds, and our hearts a portable "heaven on earth," we may more easily open the door of opportunity to experience wonderful demonstrations of Spirit in action. In the silence of the individual soul, in the sanctuary of our personal moments of prayer, we may discover that our connection with the infinite is endless. The more we focus on this inner beauty of the Creator, then, the fewer difficulties we may experience!

THE PRINCIPLE OF ATTRACTION

Albert Einstein said, "The most beautiful thing we can experience is the mysterious. It is the source of all true art and science." The universe is a mystery and humanity's inquisitiveness thrives on challenges. Scientific research is constantly unraveling more and more of the mysteries of the universe. Each discovery invites us to deeper and ever expanding research. The penetration of one mystery often uncovers an even more profound situation that may challenge our intellectual capacities. As we follow the path of investigation, we may seem to be drawn in one direction or another. What is the energy influence that catches our attention and seems to pull us in a particular direction?

The universal law or Principle of Attraction states that we often attract energies, people, and situations that are compatible with our thoughts. If we consistently think and see goodness and abundance, possibility and opportunity, for example, these elements can be drawn into our lives. If we dwell on negativity and pain and suffering, then that may be what we find. The more we dwell on any thought, the more likely it will be reflected in daily life. The proverbs "Like attracts like" and "Birds of a feather flock together" speak of the attraction that can take place between individuals, places, things, thoughts, and conditions. Can you perceive how consciousness and energy often create the nature of our personal reality?

Try this experiment. Close your eyes and imagine thousands of tiny thought particles moving around in space. Each one is glowing with the light of its particular energy vibration. For our experiment, let's consider these particles as particles of opportunity. These tiny thought particles are moving in every direction—north, south, east, west, up, down, sideways. Some may even be traveling in spirals or diagonal directions. Occasionally, two of these tiny thought particles seem drawn to each other, bump together, and, not stopping, continue in their orbit of strongest vibration. These two thought particles may meet a third and fourth and fifth thought particle of opportunity and, joining with them, form a larger vibrating unit. This unit of thought particles of opportunity may be drawn to a person who is holding an open-minded desire for greater opportunity. And a door to possibility and opportunity can open!

HOW PRACTICAL IS PURPOSE?

How can working with purpose be a practical application to help us achieve our daily needs and wants? Psychologist Abraham Maslow arranged human needs into a particular order. His viewpoint was that our basic needs of air, food, water, clothing, and shelter must be at least minimally fulfilled before we could advance toward our wants. Once the basic needs are satisfied, we can free our energies to pursue goals and desires at the next level. As Gandhi said, "Even God cannot talk to a hungry man except in terms of bread."

It is important to feel safe and secure. How can working with purpose help us accomplish this feeling? Could working with purpose
assist us in choosing worthwhile activities? It is said that an artist must
paint, a symphony conductor must conduct, a musician must make
music, a minister must minister, and a writer must write if his or her
self-worth is to be experienced as self-actualization. How can we do
what we do better each day? How can working with purpose help us
feel a greater sense of companionship and affection for those around us?

How can the decision to operate from purpose on a higher level of
awareness help us in growing, stretching, and utilizing our gifts and talents? Life has been said to be a spiral of change, a constant graceful
curve toward ongoing purpose. Could the creativity frequency possibly be one of the higher frequency capacities that our DNA cells unfold
as an aspect of the Creator, a true gift of spirit? Could this uplifting spiral be an unfolding of the golden mean ratio — into unlimited love, for
example? If the human spirit already embodies the necessary ingredi-
ents for life on Earth, does the question then become one of courage
to take action? What am I willing to do? What steps am I willing to
take? How can we make time our servant? The time taken for practical self-evaluation and identification of purposeful work is, indeed,
time well invested.

Reflections on Life

✦ What are some evidences you may have found indicating that
   purpose played a powerful role in achievement of a beneficial
   goal?

✦ Does the enthusiastic individual continually receive and release the open-minded attitude that often accompanies enthusiasm?

✦ The search for greater knowledge seems incumbent upon every human being. Education and diligent study often elevates and ennobles the human person. Could a most important avenue of research be represented by spiritual wisdom that not only enlightens the intellect, but also elevates the spirit and fosters unlimited love?

✦ How could a person's discovery of a deep spiritual truth awaken an emotion of inner joy?

PART II
FINDING THE FRUITFUL WAY

CHAPTER 4

The Humble Approach

Humility opens the door to progress.
—JOHN MARKS TEMPLETON

C AN NOBLENESS OF CHARACTER be established through the humble approach and purposeful daily living? Is the quality of daily living developed further by focusing positively and constructively on our attitudes, behaviors, choices, and actions? The responsibility for spiritual progress and for finding our purpose seems to rest almost entirely within ourselves. While enhancing the nature of our character, motives, and actions, how may we discover more of our unique attributes and intentionally direct these traits toward positive purposes?

What role does humility play in why we are here and in what good we may do? How can a humble approach to life help us experience our purpose and express real and lasting joy? Can spiritual growth and maturity take place through avenues such as the application of human reason and scientific research, through the diligent use of the various talents given to each of us, and through choosing a humble approach to research and discovery?

Are the natural world and the spiritual world two distinct, separate existences that have no relationship? Is it possible that realities perceptible to our five senses represent only a few aspects of the more fundamental spiritual realities? Unlimited love, humility, understanding, friendship, enthusiasm, loyalty, patience, mercy, noble purposes, and curiosity are but some of the spiritual realities we seek to enhance by diligent research. In taking a humble approach, could we consider this visible world an incubator provided by the Creator in which our spirits may develop and seek their greater expression in realms beyond these earthly confines?

SCHOOLROOM EARTH!

Philosophers, spiritual leaders, and other individuals often refer to Earth as a school for souls. Various major religions have also considered Earth as a school. So, how does a soul benefit in this school of life? And who and what are the teachers? Developing a humble attitude can help us overcome ignorance and self-centeredness as we increasingly use research to discover more divine realities. Learning and understanding more about a humble attitude and putting what we learn into practice can help clear our vision, provide freedom from limited values, and bring greater beauty into human life. Humility often seeks simplicity, grasps essentials, overcomes selfishness, and eliminates wasteful desires. Self-improvement frequently develops from a humble attitude.

The various "teachers" may be researched in many shapes and forms— relationships, adversity, joy, happiness, giving and receiving, self-discipline, learning to be receptive to our blessings, and gratitude. How can a person understand divine joy or be thankful for heaven on earth without previously experiencing the many challenges of earthly life? How might working for self-improvement through prayer, worship, spiritual study, and research bring beneficial discoveries?

SEEKING TO UNDERSTAND
THE BENEFITS OF HUMILITY

Is humility vastly undervalued in our modern Western culture? Is it because the meaning of the word "humility" may not be clearly understood? The term "humility" is related to the word humus and points to being connected with the Earth and, by extension, with the inhabitants of the earthly sphere. Could some people, through lack of understanding, equate humility with being passive, long-suffering, or having a sense of inferiority? In *The Perennial Philosophy,* Aldous Huxley quoted Lacordaire as saying, "Humility does not consist in hiding our talents and virtues, in thinking ourselves worse and more ordinary than we are, but in possessing a clear knowledge of all that is lacking in us and not exalting ourselves for that which we have."

The word "humility" may also mean the discovery that the Creator is infinitely beyond human comprehension and understanding. Does humility help us comprehend that humans are only tiny, temporary parts of reality, parts of a limitless, timeless Creator? By learning more about humility, might we find that the purpose of life on Earth may be far different from what most humans now suppose?

How can humility help us realize that the personal human self may be a vehicle to research and discover spiritual realities? In *World Scriptures,* we read, "Humility is an essential attitude for success in the spiritual life. Any self-conceit, whether nurtured by superior intelligence, wealth, a high position, or the praise of others, is an obstacle on the path. Genuine humility is not posturing. It requires a constant willingness to deny oneself, to be critical of oneself, and to be open to Heaven's guidance even when it differs from one's own preconceived concepts."[1]

Many spiritual and business leaders recognize that persons of true genius possess a deep sense of personal humility. The great scientist Albert Einstein maintained a strong sense of humility. He was well known for his childlike simplicity. Humility requires sincerity and honesty. Humility may be likened to the innocence of a child whose natural spontaneity and acceptance of life can be the antithesis of the more complicated adult personality.

A person makes many value choices throughout the course of a day. How can a humble attitude help us understand the greater efficiency of living that often results from the formation and development of our spiritual attributes? For example, when we develop humility as an integral part of our being, are we less motivated by ego persuasions? The person who relies upon his or her ego, skill, intelligence, or money may shut out creative inspiration and intelligence. On the other hand, does the person who is humble and grateful for each divine blessing open wider the door to heaven on Earth here and now?

If we replace being ego-centered with developing humility, can we become clearer channels for the Creator's love and wisdom to flow through us? Individual qualities may be expanded or contracted, according to our behavior. Life can be lived as a majestic and sacred adventure. And we may discover numerous adventures that indicate the active presence of divine Spirit in the world around us.

HUMILITY AS A GATEWAY TO KNOWLEDGE

Learning is a lifetime activity of vast importance. The more we learn, the more we may accomplish. The more we accomplish, the more we learn! To realize that each of us might be humbly helpful in the acceleration of creating heaven on Earth offers a glorious opportunity. Let's encourage creative thinking and beneficial action within ourselves and others. Let's humbly and enthusiastically contribute our talents to a variety of venues. The value of a questioning mind and humble service to others is not only something that is taught—it is also something that is lived!

Does humility, as a gateway to knowledge, invite us to become more open and receptive to new information? The humble approach is inherently interdisciplinary, sensitive to nuance, and favors the building of linkages and connections. It assumes openness to new ideas and an enthusiasm for research and experimentation. Humility often values patience and perseverance, honesty and integrity. As described by St. Augustine, humility helps us retain a sense of wonder and an exalted expectation: "There is something in humility which strangely exalts the heart."

If being open-minded unlocks a doorway for growth and progress, can being glad to learn represent a key that opens the door? If we think we already know it all, we are less likely to learn. While we do not need to accept every person's beliefs or ideas, we can thoughtfully examine them. We have the option to retain useful information and to release the unessential. Being open to another person's point of view might present an opportunity to discover and process new information.

The late author and astronomer Carl Sagan said, "We are rare and precious because we are alive, because we can think. We are privileged to influence and perhaps control our future." Our thinking processes greatly affect our lives. We have minds capable of creative activity in the maturation of the universe as well as in accelerating the maturation of the soul. Our ability to grow and discover new possibilities can be a powerful stimulant toward progress. Who knows what discoveries await us?

HUMILITY AS A KEY TO PROGRESS

As thanksgiving opens the door to spiritual growth, humility opens the door to progress in knowledge research and open-mindedness. When we comprehend just how little we know, we usually become ready to seek, research, and learn.

The acceleration of learning through science has brought breathtaking benefits. Could a grand opportunity lie before us through the humble approach to research about spiritual realities? For example, could cooperation between science and religion discover new avenues for creating more spiritual wealth? Our perspective plays a significant role in creating the quality of our future. Increasing our spiritual wealth can be a beneficial approach to life for all of us who desire to channel our creative energies toward helping build a heaven on Earth. Are we ready to begin expanding a humble theology that can never become obsolete?

HUMILITY THEOLOGY

Humility theology means enthusiasm for more spiritual information. To aid in this search for over one hundredfold additional spiritual discoveries, the John Templeton Foundation has expanded in scope with the formation of a research center, the Humility Theology Research Center. Major goals include sponsoring various research projects and helping form societies of respected scientists and theologians. Humility theology recognizes that *there are multiplying mysteries* and that humans may never comprehend more than a small part of reality.

Can humility be a key to our future progress and a safeguard against egotism? When a person takes a more humble approach to life, can

new spiritual ideas be welcomed the way new scientific and technological discoveries are welcomed? For example, discoveries about how
to cure infections? Or how to heat or cool the home, or how to com-
municate quickly with people who are far away?

How can we cultivate a spirit of humility? A starting point could be
allowing ourselves to be open to the possibility that our existence
within a divine reality dwarfs our personal reality. Could the spirit of
humility promote a hunger to use methods of science to research
boundless new possibilities?

HUMILITY AS A PATHWAY FOR TRANSFORMATION

The effort and means to go beyond the "ordinary" seem to character-
ize every age throughout history. Man can be described as being born
to transcend himself. As our inner and outer worlds become more
intrinsically related, the pathway to transformation begins. We reap
the harvest of what we cultivate in our life. If we focus on failure, we
often fail. If our goal involves developing an elevated consciousness, we
become more alert and aware of the things around us and of the decisions we make. Our attitudes are tremendously powerful, continu-
ously affecting all aspects of who and what we are as well as our
perceptions of the people and situations around us. Where we focus
our attention and attitudes most likely determines the degree and quality of our achievement.

An old adage of transformation tells us, "Change your attitude and
change your world." How does this work? We begin to make choices
from an uplifted perspective and a questing and productive attitude.
Purpose is energy! Purpose offers meaning and significance. Humble

purpose can represent a powerful motivating force. Life is mostly choice! As John Milton said, "The mind . . . can make a heaven into a hell, or a hell into a heaven." The power of a life that stems from inner spiritual strength is incomparable. And humility can serve as a powerful pathway toward transformation.

WHY ARE WE CREATED?

The questions "Why are we created?" and "What is the meaning of life?" are difficult to answer with the mind alone. Our intellect may help us to clarify issues and point toward progress. However, ultimately, these questions may be answered existentially through the way we live our lives. *Living on purpose* can stimulate transformation. These moments of grace and gratitude can help us acquire a humble sense of purpose and a desire to live a more fruitful life. To have an experience may be one thing; to have it affect us deeply is another.

Many of us have experienced those splendid spiritual moments when our hearts swell with an inner joy and we feel wordlessly connected to a larger source of life. We may have surrendered to the majesty of a magnificent sunset, the laughter of a child, a tender look from a loved one, or the gentle caress of the wind on our cheek. At times like these, we feel connected to the ineffable, the transcendental. Meaning and purpose go beyond mere words in a moment of spiritual discovery.

Sometimes we may be unable to measure the work we have accomplished, but progress is stamped indelibly on our souls and on the souls of those we have helped along the way. The service we humbly give to others lives beyond our days on Earth.

Spiritual Progress
through a Humble Approach to Life

Progress has long been a major goal in human thinking. People on the road toward achieving their goals take advantage of the opportunities presented. They prepare carefully for their forays into uncharted territory. They exhibit the open-minded ability to step forward into new adventures and accept challenges. They also humbly look at the experiences in their lives as conduits for greater good. The truly humble person often views others as companions upon the Earth. He or she treasures, honors, and reveres life in its abundant and magnificent forms.

The book *The Humble Approach* explores the possibility that humility in man's understanding of the Creator may be more fruitful than the formal systems of thought which we have inherited, whether they may be theistic, pantheistic, or panentheistic. We can learn to love the Creator's children and express gratitude for an increasingly rich diversity of thought emanating from worship in every land. Theological research may produce positive results even more amazing than the discoveries of scientists that have electrified the world over the last century.

Rosa Parks wrote:

Human beings are set apart from the animals. We have a spiritual self, a physical self and a conscience. Therefore, we can make choices and are responsible for the choices we make. We may choose order and peace, or confusion and chaos. If we choose the former, we may cultivate and share our talents with others. If we choose the latter, we will isolate and segregate others. We can also expand our vision to include the universe and the diversity of its people, or we can remain narrow and shallow and isolate those who are unfamiliar.[2]

How does the humble approach help us perceive that the universe and the creatures within it, both visible and invisible, may be manifestations of the eternal Creator's infinite creative purpose? What benefits can this awareness have on how we live our lives? Humility opens the door to the realms of the Spirit and to research and progress in spiritual realities. We are finding evidence of heretofore undreamed-of forces and amazing dimensions of reality that transcend the visible space-time field. Vast complexities reach out beyond the known, inspiring wonder and inviting further inquiry. Humility can open the way forward. Untold benefits may stem from frontiers of knowledge, stretching our minds far beyond the range of our present comprehension.

Through a humble attitude, how do we begin to comprehend complex perspectives of the infinity of the Creator? How does a humble approach help us expand our concepts of the Creator? How can humility help us discern from spiritual research and discovery rather than from judging by appearances? Through humility, can we avoid the sins of pride and intolerance and welcome new ideas about the Spirit? How can humility move us through a curriculum of life experiences through which we awaken into greater fullness of our potential? Who knows what discoveries might be made by proper research in the sciences of the soul!

BENEFICIAL RESULTS FROM A HUMBLE APPROACH TO LIFE

Humility helps us admit the infinity of creation and search for humanity's place in the Creator's infinite plan for creation. This approach asks each of us to personally witness the intimate relationship of physical and spiritual realities in our own life. Humbly we can use our talents to explore the universe to discover future trends. We learn to admit when we have made mistakes, to seek advice from a variety of sources, and to exert the effort to try new types of research. Learning from one another becomes a productive option. A humble approach to life invites us to be wide-eyed and open-minded enough to discover new areas for scientific research—spiritual as well as physical.

REFLECTIONS ON LIFE

✦ How can we be individual agents of creation, using the fertile ideas of our minds to enlarge the global vision of humanity?

✦ How would you describe humility as an effective gateway toward greater understanding and progress?

✦ Humility theology applauds the opportunities for more spiritual information through scientific research in both the physical and spiritual spheres.

✦ How can we learn to be humble helpers in achieving the Creator's purposes?

CHAPTER 5

The Creative Power of Purposeful Thinking

Beautiful thoughts build a beautiful soul.

—JOHN MARKS TEMPLETON

HAVE YOU HEARD the statement: "As in mind, so in manifestation"? Or, "Your thoughts create your world"? Or, "Everything originates in the mind"? Our thoughts are vital energies that often influence how we live our lives. Our thoughts also affect our relationships with others. They often can impact the contributions we make to our world.

Can we change the texture of the mental "fabric" of our minds? Can we monitor the way we think and respond to everyday experiences? How vital is becoming the master custodian of the way we think? In *What Are You?* Imelda Shanklin writes:

> Your thoughts are the tools with which you carve your life story on the substance of the universe. When you rule your mind you rule your world. When you choose your thoughts you choose results. The visible part of your life pours out of your mind, shaped and stamped by your thoughts, as surely as the coins of nations are shaped and stamped by the mechanisms used to convert ores into specie.[1]

The good news is that we can do something constructive and beneficial about the way we think. We can choose the quality of our thoughts and feelings. Inherent within these choices, the opportunities arise to create vital, healthy, and beneficial patterns of living. What is the connection between the caliber of our thinking and the conditions existing in the world? How might our lives change if we refuse to dwell on any thought in our minds that we would not wish to see objectified in our lives? How are your present thoughts contributing to your life's purpose?

WHAT ARE THOUGHTS?

In *Awakening to Zero Point*, Gregg Braden describes thought in this way. "Thought may be considered as an energy of scalar potential, the directional seed of an expression of energy that may, or may not, materialize as a real or vector event. A virtual assembling of your experience, thought provides the guidance system, the direction, for where the energy of your attention may be directed."[2] He defines "scalar potential" as a quality of energy that has not been dispersed or dissipated, or energy filled with potential and waiting to be used.

Thinking represents one aspect of consciousness. Thought cannot exist without consciousness. However, does consciousness require thought? What do we mean by this statement? Our thoughts require energy to become empowered. Considering the definition that thought may be identified as a guidance system, a directional program for the energy that we contribute to our world, how can the process of thinking propel us toward our purpose?

If we could use an instrument that recorded our thinking processes for a day and then played those thoughts back to us, we might be surprised to learn why things may go amiss and activities can become snarled. An experience of this nature might inspire us with creative incentives to strengthen our minds with positive, loving, and constructive habits of thinking. So, rather than reacting to situations and circumstances, we may choose to develop skills to express initiative and creative and beneficial responses.

In his novel, *La Réponse de Seigneur*, Alphonse de Châteaubriant compares the human mind to a butterfly that assumes the color of the foliage on which it settles. "We become what we contemplate," he wrote. If our minds are preoccupied with non-productive thoughts such as worry, concern, gossip, failure, or resentment, then our thoughts are colored with these hues. If our focus is on positive traits such as joy, unlimited love, service, divine purposes, enthusiasm, diligence, and usefulness, the mind's hue again responds. Centuries earlier, Marcus Aurelius made a similar observation when he said, "Such as are thy habitual thoughts, such also will be the character of thy soul —for the soul is dyed by thy thoughts."[3]

OUR THOUGHTS DEFINE OUR WORLD

Our thoughts can accomplish a great deal more than coloring our mind. Beautiful thoughts contribute to building a beautiful soul. "Our thoughts define our world" is a powerful universal principle at work in our lives—mentally, physically, and spiritually. As we observe the possibilities, dimensions, and applications of a thought, it tends to become more clearly defined. Thoughts become clothed in emotions and the new thinking and feeling energy becomes part of our attitude. Through directed practice, we can visualize and strengthen particular ideas and bring them into manifestation in our lives. By focusing our thoughts on love, strength, joy, or humility, we can create more love, strength, joy, and humility in our lives.

Because of the increasing rapidity with which science and technology are changing, we may find ourselves making choices—with accompanying consequences—that will produce effects for many years. For the first time in recorded history, we have the science and technology to accomplish things never before considered. For example, we can now modify our climate and change the balance of nature in ways that were unimaginable only a generation ago.

Are we egotistical to ignore the mathematicians who suggest that reality may have as many as eleven dimensions rather than three dimensions plus time? How do we think and feel about the technology that enables us to create new forms of life and copy those already existing? Is today's reality vastly more complex than we have yet comprehended? Are we moving beyond those mind patterns and thinking processes that dominated human life for eons of time? Has our science grown faster than our wisdom in applying these findings to everyday living in responsible ways? How can we stay abreast of this quantum leap in the evolution of human consciousness? How can we know which choices will be most fruitful and beneficial?

Taking a closer look at questions regarding how the creative power of purposeful thinking operates in our life offers a good starting point. How can we develop more positive interpretations of the people, the events, and the world around us? How can thinking positively help us learn from difficulties? What is the relationship between focus, perseverance, diligence, purpose, and mastering our thoughts? How can observation of our thought processes open up timeless dimensions? How often is our attention focused on the past or on the future rather than in the now moment? How may we acquire freedom from useless, unnecessary thinking by observing our own thought processes? Also, does another factor figure in — the witnessing presence of infinite intelligence, what some call Divine Mind? Our search can begin by looking within.

YOU ARE MORE THAN YOUR MIND

In his book *The Power of Now,* Eckhart Tolle tells the following story:

> A beggar had been sitting by the side of the road for over thirty years. One day a stranger walked by.
>
> "Spare some change?" mumbled the beggar, mechanically holding out his old baseball cap.
>
> "I have nothing to give you," said the stranger. Then he asked: "What's that you are sitting on?"
>
> "Nothing," replied the beggar. "Just an old box. I have been sitting on it for as long as I can remember."
>
> "Ever looked inside?" asked the stranger.
>
> "No," said the beggar. "What's the point? There's nothing in there."
>
> "Have a look inside," insisted the stranger. The beggar proceeded to pry open the lid of the box. With astonishment, disbelief, and elation, he saw that the box was filled with gold.[4]

The moral of this story invites us to look within ourselves and discover an invisible reservoir of abundant potential. New revelations regarding many areas of our lives may be ours if we open our minds to inquiry and research. Some people have considered our true nature to be a state of being, a manifestation of divine energy that is immeasurable and indestructible. Is this divinity the eternal presence that includes the myriad forms of life that are subject to birth and death? Paradoxically, divinity may be our innermost invisible and indestructible essence. Could we then surmise that this creative energy is the basic reality of our own deepest selves, our true nature?

Emanuel Swedenborg wrote that nothing exists separate from God. He also taught that God is all of us and we are a little part of God. We are daily swimming in an ocean of unseen potential and possibilities. Each living cell represents a miracle of life and the human body houses a vast colony of over a hundred billion cells. The living miracle of our bodies includes both our ability to recognize, as well as our inability to exhaust, the true significance of who and what we are. The human being is even more awe inspiring than the billions of stars in the universe.

BODY/BRAIN/MIND CONNECTION

Is one of the Creator's most marvelous and mysterious creations on earth the human brain, with its indwelling ability to be creative and purposeful? With our minds, are we able to participate in small ways in the creation of matter and even in life itself? The human mind has been described as a thought-processing system that is intricately linked to the physical brain. Possibly, the brain registers thoughts electrically on the physical level. The mind experiences thought directly on the level of conscious awareness. The mind, or this thought-processing system, can be a superb instrument when used humbly and beneficially. Used selfishly or negatively, it can become a destructive instrument. Thus, a key element of living fruitfully and successfully may be to recognize the mind as an instrument to be directed and used for the highest and best good.

The companionable workings of the human body, brain, and mind can explain certain events in a person's life. But how do we explain some of the mysteries that occur on a deeper level? Why have people throughout history and from so many different cultures sought and worshipped something unseen and beyond human comprehension? What guides us to recognize which avenue of action may be beneficial while another may be destructive? What prompts a person to take the coat from his back on a wintry day to give to an old person who has no coat?

Does a vast realm of intelligence exist beyond human thought, with thought representing only a tiny aspect of that intelligence? How do we account for the layers of infinite intellectual order—not yet discovered by humans—beneath the surface of everyday phenomena? Do many of us have an innate sense of the infinite intellect and become inspired to think, feel, and do the things that maintain harmony and productivity? Are the things that really matter—such as unlimited love, compassion, joy, beauty, honor, integrity, and truth—really deeper states of spiritual consciousness that arise from beyond what we call "the human mind"?

CONSCIOUSNESS

In the nineteenth century, Edwin A. Abbott wrote a small book titled *Flatland*. A. Square, the narrator, tells a story of a land populated by a large number of Squares and Circles, with a subculture of Triangles and an occasional Parallelogram. In Flatland, the citizens lived in two dimensions, seeing and knowing only what could be seen and known in that plane and unaware of anything above or below it. Although fearful at first, A. Square developed the ability to ask questions and look beyond his present consciousness. He began to see deeper. He saw marvelous Cones and sparkling Cylinders. And, oh my, there was even a Great Sphere made up of Triangles that was called a Geodesic Dome! As the story unfolds, A. Square begins to realize that his experiences in Flatland represented only a small part of the larger picture.

Are we, too, recognizing that there are multiplying evidences of purpose in the universe and in creativity? *Flatland* offers a provocative analogy to the world we inhabit. Whether scientific, philosophical, or theological, how can we expand our minds and thought processes to better know the great plan and purposes of which we are a part?

Beneath the wave of our human consciousness lies the infinite ocean of the Creator's consciousness. Does the human wave occasionally forget it is a part of the greater ocean and "isolate" itself from the oceanic power? Because of this "forgetfulness," can our thought processes become weakened or restricted by a sense of limitations?

The seeds of success abide within us. Seeds may appear small. Yet, within a tiny seed resides the blueprint of an enormous tree, with towering trunk and heavy, outspread branches that can provide a home for nesting birds or shade for weary travelers. The potential within the seed, by itself, does not produce the tree. The seed must be planted in the ground and given water and fertilizer and nurturing to become the young sapling that grows into the magnificent tree. A life-changing seed of thought may be lying quietly within each of us, waiting to be nurtured and developed!

WHAT ABOUT "REALITY"?

In *The Spectrum of Consciousness,* Ken Wilber wrote:

Since modes of knowing correspond with levels of consciousness, and since Reality is a particular mode of knowing, it follows that Reality is a level of consciousness. . . . Reality is what is revealed from the non-dual level of consciousness that we have termed Mind. That it is revealed is a matter of experimental fact; what is revealed however, cannot be accurately described without reverting to the symbolic mode of knowing."[5]

Could our present human perception of reality be as meager as a clam's perceptions of humans? Is there evidence that human perceptions of reality are accelerating? Why? How? Could we discover more if we use the word "reality" to mean the totality of appearances plus fundamentals? We may discuss what reality is like, what it is not, and speculate on how we may discover more, but presently, our language seems inadequate to describe the scope of reality.

Should the human ego, or should the lack of egotistical attitudes, be considered a level of consciousness? The minds that are continually seeking to discover new insights and new perspectives can research many questions to glean new information. The questing mind can research the wonders of the universe. The open mind is unafraid to challenge old assumptions or to compete with others in creative professional competition. When the open-minded thinker's concepts falter or break down, new hypotheses for testing can be devised.

The spectrum of consciousness seems vast and we can weave in and out of numerous levels of thinking and consciousness in the space of a day. If we tried to set one level of thinking apart from another level, would we be imposing some limitation on the mind? If we look at our everyday state of consciousness, whether it be sad, happy, agitated, calm, peaceful, or fearful, can we consider these expressions as simply being where we are at a particular moment? What are the beneficial results when we choose to "come up a little higher"?

THOUGHT AS A KEY
TO EXPANDING SPIRITUAL DISCOVERIES

Data available from research programs financed through the Templeton Foundation frequently suggests that vast resources of mind may be
accessible if various methods of testing are researched carefully and sci-
entifically. Experiences of penetrating insight, the sudden appearance
of solutions to seemingly intractable scientific problems, the incredible creativity that musical and mathematical inspiration often entails,
and the sense of the presence of awesome force are often seen as essential spiritual "happenings" by the people who experience them. Is there
a mystical force or energy that transcends the faculties of the intellect
and, likewise, the human body? How can we better understand this
intuition, impulse, or prompting that, instead of happening occasionally, could become our natural, even frequent, experience?

How do these kinds of experiences correlate with our thought
processes? How can these experiences, which are so valuable to the
individuals involved, be extended to a much wider spectrum of soci-
ety? Are our minds capable of helping in the creative activity of the
universe as well as in the growth and search for purpose of the human
soul? How important is it for each of us to keep our focus strongly
linked to our soul's purpose and our soul linked to the Creator? In this
way, can the creative process in which we engage flow from the mind
of divinity through our souls to our minds, where creative thinking
can produce creative results in the physical world? Could this activity
be described as coming into a greater fullness and expression of the
Spirit of infinite creativity?

Through creative thinking, may we experience divine intelligence
effecting changes in the visible culture that we create within our

homes, families, schools, churches, businesses, and governments? May we also become increasingly aware of personal spiritual growth? If thoughts held in our minds are tremendously powerful, does every helpful thought have a literal value?

Ralph Waldo Trine said, "The higher forces of the inner life, those of the mind and spirit, always potential within, become of actual value only as they are recognized, realized, and used."[6] Does growing in spiritual consciousness help open up limited thinking patterns that have dominated humans for eons of time and created untold restriction and conflict?

MANAGING YOUR THOUGHTS

Could benefits to the human brain be greatly enhanced if appropriate methods were discovered for mobilizing the remaining unused neural networks? Is this possibility supported, in part, by the limited data available on the people termed "idiot savants," who exhibit remarkable abilities in mathematics or music although their general abilities may be quite limited? Do some of these findings imply that the human brain can perform incredible functions under particular conditions? Could spiritual attributes also be enhanced by diligent research, thus leading to the accelerated spiritual development of humankind?

While many excellent avenues of mental explorations invite further scientific research, what can we do now, in this moment, to enhance our thinking processes? As we recognize the truth that "thoughts are things," as we discover that thoughts are more important, or at least equally as important as feelings and actions, can we take a giant step toward becoming masters of our minds and toward achieving our purposes? Could changing the focus of our thoughts promote better physical, mental, and spiritual health? How can we guard the doorway of our minds to help our thoughts, words, and actions to be congruent with our goals, vision, and purpose?

RENEWING THE MIND

Is there anything more difficult in life than the acceptance of a new idea when tradition restricts our viewpoint? The laws of the mind are stringent. As mentioned earlier, the human experience, individually and collectively, is the result of our consciousness. And consciousness represents the sum total of our subjective and objective impressions and awareness. Perhaps "renewing" our minds could provide many beneficial opportunities.

The parable of the cloth and the wineskins offers good instructions for letting go of negative thought patterns and replacing them with new, vitalizing, and spiritually positive thoughts. In Matthew 9:17 we read: "Neither is new wine put into old wineskins; otherwise the skins burst, and the wine is spilled, and the skins are destroyed, but new wine is put into fresh wineskins, and so both are preserved." How can this parable stimulate our minds and awaken our senses to higher possibilities? From this elevated perspective, we can observe people and the world around us, hear the sounds of joyful enthusiasm, and feel the resonance of love and goodwill. When we renew our minds by changing our present mode of thinking, do we parallel the analogy of putting new wine into new wineskins?

As we become purposeful guardians of our thoughts, we take advantage of the opportunity to observe the possibilities, dimensions, and applications of an idea until it becomes more clearly defined in our minds. With practice, we can create, visualize, and strengthen a new idea by placing our focus on it, then take further steps to experiment with the benefits of the idea. Saint Teresa said, "As soon as you apply yourself to reflection, you will feel at once your senses gather themselves together; they seem like bees which return to the hive and there shut themselves up to work at the making of honey."

Positive mental qualities may take time to develop. Humble dedication and perseverance is often required. Continued reflective focus and enthusiasm to experiment may be simple and effective keys toward beautiful thoughts building a beautiful mind. Using the mind for higher purposes results in more fruitful experiences.

THE THINKING/FEELING CONNECTION

"Emotion" has been described as energy in motion. Another definition states that emotions are feeling reactions to a particular situation that impacts all the parts of someone's personality. If everything is formed from energy vibrations, our thoughts and feelings may be thought of as powerful energy frequencies. Scientists, measuring various areas or frequencies of the brain, have found that different states of thought and feeling produce wave frequencies called alpha, beta, theta, or delta. Since we have a choice in how we think and feel, in essence, we can choose our frequencies!

Is there a difference between "emotion" and "feeling"? Some people and dictionaries consider the two words interchangeable, using each one to define the other. *Webster's New World College Dictionary* defines emotion as: "a state of consciousness having to do with the arousal of feelings, distinguished from other mental states, as cognition and awareness of physical sensation." Feeling is defined as "the power or faculty of experiencing physical sensations."

Possibly one difference between feeling and emotion is that intense emotion can become emotionalism, representing an indulgence in unbalanced emotion. The role of emotions, in some instances, may have been overemphasized in its importance to the psychological life. Emotionalism does not usually solve problems, while sincere feelings like unlimited love or forgiveness can bridge immense chasms. While emotions may affect parts of our personalities, we are not at their mercy. We have the option of refocusing our emotional perspective from the body or mind to the inner realm of Spirit. As we continue to learn about the thought/feeling connection, we begin to build a more efficient and effective relationship between these two vital aspects of life. Thoughts and feelings may then become tools, encoded with light, power, and intelligence, to help us re-create and purposefully manage our lives. Ideas clothed with zeal and enthusiasm can accelerate us on the path toward our goals and purposes.

Emotions and feelings, in their many and varied expressions, determine to a point how we experience life. Research demonstrates that specific feelings produce predictable chemical reactions in our bodies that correspond to a particular feeling. What happens when your thoughts become anxious and fearful? Do your hands feel cold and clammy? Does your breathing feel tight and restricted? Have you observed someone else or yourself when angry? What happens? In many instances, the body becomes flushed. Drops of perspiration may form on the brow and around the mouth. Facial muscles tense and tighten. The eyes flash. Heartbeat speeds up. And, importantly, the mind may momentarily go into overload and lose some ability for coherent thinking.

On the other hand, feelings of love and compassion bring relaxation and play a role in optimizing our immune systems and the regulatory functions of our bodies. Used appropriately and beneficially, our emotions and feelings can elevate us to new heights of joyous living. When ignored or wrongly directed, they contribute to making living a miserable experience.

LISTENING WITH PURPOSE

The art of listening is an important beneficial element of purposeful thinking. Immense value may be found in listening carefully, thoughtfully, and appreciatively to everyone's ideas. An old saying reminds us that the Creator gave us two ears and one mouth so we could hear more and talk less! How well we listen can play an important part in determining what we learn as we travel on the journey of life.

In some instances, we may get so caught up in planning our response that we overlook the opportunity to hear what the other person may be saying. Allowing ourselves the opportunity to assimilate what we hear before responding is important and beneficial. Frank Tyger said, "Hearing is one of the body's five senses. But listening is an art!"[7] When listening to what someone is saying, consider listening with your entire body! Feel the energy that is clothed with words and flowing from the other person's thoughts.

Have you considered listening as a viable way of improving relationships? A good listener helps keep lines of communication open. Effective communication represents an important skill for successful and useful living. A beneficial exercise to try is to concentrate on what the other person is saying and feeling. Then, when you respond in the conversation, begin your sentence with "you" instead of "I." You may be surprised at how much you learn!

When we listen with spiritual intent and purpose, we draw upon resources that go far beyond our human capabilities. As we tap this higher resource and act upon its inspiration, we develop the ability to respond in beneficial, constructive, and creative ways to every situation. Listening is a learned skill; when developed to the fullest degree, it helps increase our capacity to learn, provides opportunities to expand our creative talents, and enhances our ability to maintain healthy relationships.

Active listening necessitates staying focused on what the person who is speaking is saying. In active listening, we use our ears in a similar way to a photographer using a camera. To get the best pictures, the photographer adjusts the lens of the camera until the settings capture a clear picture. As active listeners, we adjust the focus of our attention to remain aware of what the speaker is saying. The more we listen and learn, the better we are able to develop our innate potential.

REFLECTIONS ON LIFE

✦ How would you describe "reality" as a level of consciousness? Are the intellectual/rational mind and the spiritually oriented mind separate states of consciousness? Or could they be considered harmonious parts of the whole?

✦ How would your life unfold and progress with greater purpose if you decided to meet petulance with patience, hatred with unlimited love, judgment with forgiveness, criticism and dissent with compassionate kindness, and questioning with an open mind. Could you live eagerly and enthusiastically, doing the kindly deeds that express heartfelt joy in service to others?

✦ Are we here to be motivated throughout our lives, from youth to the older years, by an insatiable curiosity about everything? Are we also here to genuinely, humbly, and enthusiastically help others, especially by building our own potential and purposes?

CHAPTER 6

The Greatness of the Loving Heart

. . . and the greatest of these is love.

—I CORINTHIANS 13:13

Love may possibly be one of the most written about, talked about, sung about, and over- and under-described subjects on earth! Possibly no other word has been given so many definitions in poetry, plays, novels, and philosophical and theological texts as "love."

The Greeks developed several definitions of love. Romantic love was called *eros*, the kind of emotional love that can put butterflies in your stomach. *Storge* is the type of love that we feel for members of our family. It is sometimes referred to as the love of security. *Phileo*, companionship, represents the type of love we feel for our friends. However, perhaps the more important and life-enhancing love is what the Greeks called *agape*.

Agape is the unselfish love that gives without limit and expects nothing in return. It is the love that grows as we give it to others. In fact, the more agape love we give, the more we have left to give. Agape is the kind of love that great spiritual teachers such as Jesus, Buddha, Muhammad, Lao Tzu, Confucius, and others taught us to practice. Agape is holy, unconditional, unchanging, permanent, and unlimited love. This miraculous love is ever present and available for everyone! Its source doesn't depend on external factors because agape represents a state of being. It is a caring, forgiving, nurturing, and supportive way of relating to everyone.

Mother Teresa described love as the central point of our existence. She wrote, "For this purpose we have been created: to love and be loved."[1] Do her words represent a level of development where love encourages us to be "one with another"? Can unlimited love progressively expand our sense of self and others and encourage us to focus on the goodness of life in its variety of expressions? Does this quality of love augment positive expressions and dissolve negativity—not by attacking negativity, but rather by loving it into wholeness?

IS UNLIMITED LOVE A PRIMARY PURPOSE?

Is it possible that love really is a primary purpose for our existence in earth? We seem more fulfilled when we are in a state of spiritual love and, somehow, less fruitful and effective when our focus moves elsewhere. Could our souls have been conceived in the Creator's unlimited love and could this love foreshadow our purpose? Are the love, kindness, and patience that we bring to our relationships ways to be in touch with spiritual discoveries? Is the Law of Love a transformational law that brings heaven to earth through the movement of unlimited love?

In *Divine Love and Wisdom*, Emanuel Swedenborg wrote:

Some idea of love, as being the life of man, may be had from the sun's heat in the world. This heat is well known to be the common life, as it were, of all the vegetation of the earth. For by virtue of heat, coming forth in springtime, plants of every kind rise from the ground, deck themselves with leaves, then with blossoms, and finally, with fruits, and thus, in a sense, live. But when, in the time of autumn and winter, heat withdraws, the plants are stripped of these signs of their life, and they wither. So it is with love in man; for heat and love mutually correspond. Therefore, love is also warm.[2]

The sun of our solar system has been described as a self-sustaining unit whose energy source is derived from internal thermonuclear reactions. Scientists tell us the energy released in these reactions is so vast that the sun could shine for millions of years with little change in its size or brightness. Does an analogy between the strength, power, light, warmth, and wisdom of unlimited love correlate with the radiance of our solar system's sun? Especially with the knowledge that invisible electromagnetic energy fields surround all living things. Both the sun and unlimited love bring life-giving warmth and light to a planet and its people.

Could unlimited love be described as a creative, sustaining energy? When we embrace our creative energy, can we draw, from the universal Source, a tremendous spiritual energy matrix into many areas of our lives? Does a divine fountainhead of love exist in the universe in which degrees of human participation are possible?

THE EXTRAORDINARY POTENTIAL AND BENEFITS OF UNLIMITED LOVE

Scholars throughout the ages have defined love as a unifying power that joins and binds everything in the universe. Love has also been described as the greatest harmonizing principle known to man. Lope de Vega observed, "Harmony is pure love, for love is complete agreement." When we discover the miracle of unlimited love and explore its deeper meaning, how could there be disharmony between us and another?

Some people may be afraid to love because they fear being hurt, rejected, or feeling the pain of a "broken heart." Can these responses result from habitual emotional patterns that short-circuit our minds and emotions? Does holding on to real or perceived hurts or resentments only cause feelings of self-victimization and additional pain? How can we connect with the greatness of our loving hearts, resolve these situations in our minds, release the aching pain, and move forward? How can we build greater "heart strength" and learn from these experiences?

While the expression "unlimited love" resonates closely with the ideal of agape love, it seems to be more appealing to many people than a technical, theological term from ancient Greece. Also, unlimited love is a title free of association with any one religious faith tradition and can appeal across cultures and academic disciplines. Unlimited love can be representative of the ultimate nature of love as a spiritual and creative influence.

By definition, "unlimited" means without limit or restriction. Unlimited love can describe love for humanity and perhaps, on a less ontological level, love for all living creatures. Unlimited love can mean we allow no insulating boundaries to be drawn to separate us from others. Could research and progress in learning more about unlimited love move humanity forward to a more fruitful, constructive, expressive, and beneficial future?

The great paradox of unlimited love may be that it calls on us to express our spiritual selves fully and honestly. Unlimited love has the ability to look at the whole as well as at a fragment of any situation. Unlimited love can take into consideration the existence, needs, and points of view of those involved in a given situation. Unlimited love releases bindings of guilt or expectation. It cannot be bought or sold or reduced to any kind of commodity.

Unlimited love, as with any other spiritual virtue, needs to be cultivated into its fully expressed and beautiful reality. How can individuals learn to love in a more conscious, unlimited way? One guideline would be to give more of our attention to loving unconditionally and in an unlimited manner. Explore what unconditional love means. Is it love without judgments? Consider the various facets and aspects of unlimited love. Increasingly notice the acts of kindness and compassion demonstrated by others. Look for the loving presence. Let's also remind ourselves how much we have to give! Practice the universal principle of giving and receiving, joyously and humbly. Find joy in the spiritual quality of thoughts, words, and actions. Look for opportunities to give love and compassion. Visualize unlimited love in expression and develop greater attunement with the quality you are picturing in your mind. The experience of the presence of the Creator is within and available to each of us at all times.

Unlimited love may be regarded as an essence of divine goodness and inseparable from other spiritual qualities. This kind of love can provide considerable energy to creating the highest values of human life. For example, love enhances the richness of truth, knowledge, beauty, freedom, goodness, and happiness. These beneficial values tangibly affect, enrich, change, and ennoble individuals, groups, nations, and the course of human history. So, would it not be beneficial for us to direct our focus toward expressing unlimited love and guide our thoughts, feelings, decisions, and actions to stem from this magnanimous love?

What can happen when we choose unlimited love over lesser egotistical and materialistic goals?

In *The Ways and Power of Love*, Pitirim A. Sorokin described love in this way:

> More concretely, love is the experience that annuls our individual loneliness; fills the emptiness of our isolation with the richest value; breaks and transcends the narrow walls of our little egos; makes us coparticipants in the highest life of humanity and in the whole cosmos; expands our true individuality to the immeasurable boundaries of the universe.[3]

SERVICE AS LOVE IN ACTION

How can we learn to be helpers in the Creator's purposes? Along with the gift of individuality that the Creator has so generously provided for each of us, we have also received the priceless gift of personal free will. Why are we gifted with such creativity and possibilities? And, having the right of self-determination, what shall we do with our lives and with this dynamic ability? Could a key response to these questions lie in realizing that the Creator has superb purposes for our lives?

As we contemplate and experience the creative spirit of unlimited love, are we likely to feel a deep desire to attune ourselves more fully with the Creator's will for the universe and its inhabitants? Could we gratefully ask, "Infinite Spirit, in what ways may I be of service for your divine plan for humanity?" Spiritual progress may include growth and advancement in a variety of fields of endeavor. For example, using scientific exploration and studies to gain greater understanding of the Creator may constitute a form of spiritual progress.

Service has sometimes been described as love in action. And, paradoxically, loving service offers a powerful tool for implementing our own spiritual growth. When our thoughts are turned toward service, we often cease to grasp and become more receptive. Could an affective guideline for daily living be: Do the most you can with what you have in the present moment?

Scripture tell us "It is better to give than to receive" (Acts 20:35). How can the talents, abilities, intelligence, and success with which we are blessed be returned to the world in some form that will benefit humanity? Unselfish giving can be a sign of personal and spiritual maturity. Giving leads to greater giving and becomes a way of life. When you give of your talents and abilities, can you see how your personal sense of thanksgiving, gratitude, and spiritual accomplishment expands as well?

Few diseases seem so childish and so deadly as the "gimmies." A grasping spirit reflects an attitude that can isolate us from family and friends. The secret of success is giving, not getting. To get joy, we must give joy, and to keep joy, we must scatter it. Perhaps one of the greatest charities is that of helping a person understand and eliminate the destructive power of the "gimmies" and learn to become a loving giver.

LOVE AND HUMILITY: HOW ARE THEY RELATED?

If we endorse a humble approach to life, do we radiate love and happiness as faithfully as the sun radiates light and warmth? As sunlight is a creative source, in like manner, can unlimited love serve as a creative source for discovering new ideas? If we release egotistical self-will and invite the richness of divine love into our lives, do we become more effective channels for the Creator's love and wisdom?

This is a wonderful blossoming time for humanity. Evolution is accelerating. Progress is accelerating. We could even perceive the acceleration of change in our world as contributing to our many blessings. We live in a time when developing suitable methods of scientific inquiry into spiritual matters could be tremendously beneficial. What insights might be gleaned from research that explores the spiritual foundations of effective living? What could we learn from researching divine qualities and virtues—such as unlimited love and humility— that benefit the lives of individuals and societies? What grand opportunities abound for unlimited love and humility to open the doors to exciting research into the science of the soul? Who knows, the spirit of unlimited love and humility, which we build during our lifetimes, may be that part of the human person that is immortal! Radiant, unlimited love, universal, eternal!

UNLIMITED LOVE AS HEALING ENERGY

How do giving and receiving love enhance our capabilities of promoting health, preventing disease, prolonging life, and hastening recovery? Over recent decades, scientists have systematically explored links between the mind and body and new scientific fields have evolved accordingly. Could further research involving the range of determinants of health and disease be expanded to include things like our thoughts, feelings, motivations, personalities, and interactions with others? Do loving and feeling loved provide a sense of order and offer reassurances of more positive outcomes? Can believing that we are loved, especially by the Creator, create a sense of optimism and hope that may be physiologically beneficial? How might scientific research confirm this possibility? How could discoveries from this type of research affect our unfolding purposes?

In *Power Through Constructive Thinking*, Emmet Fox writes:

There is no difficulty that enough love will not conquer; no dis-ease that enough love will not heal; no door that enough love will not open; no gulf that enough love will not bridge; no wall that enough love will not throw down; no wrong that enough love will not set right; it makes no difference how deeply seated may be the trouble; how helpless the outlook; how muddled the tangle; how great the mistake; a sufficient realization of love will dissolve it all—if only you will love enough, you will be the hap-piest, most powerful being in the world.[4]

What could happen if we merged these thoughts of love with our daily activities?

If we focused our thoughts on health and wholeness and immersed our emotions in unlimited love, could healing be a natural result? Someone described the healing energy of love as a spiritual antibody that helps eliminate disease in the human body. As we learn to be more loving and forgiving, unlimited love and forgiveness can influence our mental, emotional, and physical health. We might discover greater con-text and increased perspective in working toward our purposes.

THE WAYS OF LOVE

Do we presently know and understand less about "the energy of love" than we do about light, heat, electricity, and other forms of physical energy? Abraham Maslow said, "It is amazing how little the empirical sciences have to offer on the subject of love." At the present juncture of our human history, has an increase in our knowledge of unlimited love become a paramount need of humanity?

In *The Ways and Power of Love*, Pitirim Sorokin considers several aspects of love. The religious aspect of love identifies love with a higher presence, however variously symbolized in the great spiritual and religious traditions. The ethical aspect of love identifies love with goodness itself. The ontological aspect of love defines it as "a unifying, integrating, harmonizing, creative energy or power" that works in the physical, organic, and psychosocial worlds. The physical aspect of love is shown in "all the forces that unite, integrate, and maintain the whole inorganic cosmos in endless unity, beginning with the smallest unity of the atom and ending with the whole physical universe as one unified, orderly cosmos."[5] Personal lives and a variety of social conditions seem to be far more fluid than we may realize. For example, look at your own life. How different are you now from the person you were ten years ago? Five years ago? Perhaps even one year ago? How might Sorokin's ideas about the aspects of love contribute to your present reality? Are you aware of a spiritual maturing process that may be happening in your thoughts, feelings, and actions? As we learn to love more, do we engage a higher frequency range of our hearts' qualities and quicken our intuitive connection with Spirit? Could unlimited love be described, in one aspect, as a cosmic energy in which human participation is possible? Does such love produce health and peace in our world and aid and participate in humanity's purpose? Could unlimited love, unbounded in its extensity, maximal in its intensity, purity, duration, and adequacy, and inseparable from universal truth and divinity, offer humanity a high moral value around which other positive values can be harmoniously integrated?

Could putting into practice a greater understanding of the quality of unlimited love be reflected in our lives as higher demonstrations of brain/mind consciousness?

CAN LOVE BE AN ETERNAL UNIVERSAL FORCE MORE POTENT THAN GRAVITY, LIGHT, OR ELECTROMAGNETISM?

Physicists like Albert Einstein openly and movingly spoke of the religious attitude as essential to good science. Sir James Jeans said that the universe was beginning to look not like a great machine but rather like a great thought. Astronomer Allen Sandage spoke of God in terms of the marvelous laws of nature, and Sir Arthur Eddington once wrote of a spiritual world that lies behind the universe we study. In *The Future of Man*, Teilhard de Chardin wrote, "'Love one another, recognizing in the heart of each of you the sure God who is being born.' Those words, first spoken two thousand years ago, now begin to reveal themselves as the essential structural law of what we call progress and evolution. They enter the scientific field of cosmic energy and its necessary laws."[6]

Certainly, there seems to be no conclusive argument for design and purpose, but there are strong evidences of ultimate reality more fundamental than the cosmos. So, if there are phenomenal universal forces, for example, in gravity, in the light spectrum, or in electromagnetism, can there not also be a tremendous unknown or non-researched potency or force in unlimited love? With earthly information now doubling every three years, can our comprehension of some of these intangibles of spirit also be multiplied more than one hundredfold? Could unlimited love be an aspect of dimensions beyond what we presently know as time and space? Could unlimited love be a universal concept beyond matter and energy as they are currently understood? To what realms beyond the physical might unlimited love reach? Just how vast is the reach of unlimited love?

Rumi wrote, "Love is the energizing elixir of the universe, the cause and effect of all harmonies." Our energy fields are electrical in nature and may be measured with sophisticated measuring devices. The scientific community refers to the energy fields surrounding all living things as electromagnetic waves.

As we research for deeper levels of the eternal universal force of unlimited love, can the results we experience from an increased quality of life motivate us into wider dimensional awareness? Would a natural evolution of this increasing awareness result in greater clarity about our purposes and why we are here? How does our perspective, at any given moment, play a significant part in creating the quality of our future? What are your spiritual views of reality?

Albert Einstein was fond of contrasting his mathematics with his spiritual views of reality. He stated, "I want to know how God created this world. I want to know his thoughts, the rest are details."[7] The faces of reality are changing daily. The manifold scientific discoveries of the last century seem to cause the visible and tangible to appear less real and point to a greater reality in the ongoing and accelerating creative process within the enormity of the basic unseen. Many of us are still searching for that deeper meaning and for a cosmic explanation of ourselves and our purposes. Changes in human understanding may occur in simple as well as in complex ways. Sometimes the movements of our thoughts appear to be going in several directions at once as we seek greater clarity through our study. So, we continue to ask questions.

THE IMPORTANCE OF ASKING QUESTIONS

Einstein seemed to view God as dressed in questions more than answers. Questions can be an invitation to greater awareness. They often point us toward areas of our experience that need attention. When we allow the question that is implicit in our difficulty to become explicit, we are inviting our awareness to enter the situation and offer guidance. Many of the questions we ask about ultimate reality and purpose and meaning may be searching, exploratory, and tentative, but they are often profound as well. From this perspective we ask additional questions, such as: Are our human concepts of God too small? Are they too human-centered? Does a tiny wave that is a temporary manifestation of the ocean of which it is a part resemble our relationship to the Creator?

It is hoped that you, the reader, may find that the questions asked in this small book can stir your imagination, stimulate expanding thought processes, and perhaps encourage your own further research and exploration. As we begin to perceive and better understand our limitations as finite creatures in a vast universe of infinite complexity and intricacy, perhaps we can be released from our prejudices — whether scientific, philosophical, or religious — and open our minds to study the great plan of which we are a part.

REFLECTIONS ON LIFE

✦ What benefits could result from sincerely saying to others, "God loves you and so do I"?

✦ Is agape love a product of the human mind, or can human minds be a product of pure, limitless, timeless love, which some call God?

✦ Is it possible to give too much divine love?

✦ How can we distinguish the ardor of giving too many goods or instructions (which can retard maturity) from divine love, which helps the receiver to gain the joy of giving?

✦ How do the following lines from Alexander Pope's *Essay on Man* speak to you about unlimited love?

> God loves from whole to parts: but human soul
> Must rise from individual to the whole.
> Self-love but serves the virtuous mind to wake,
> As the small pebble stirs the peaceful lake;
> The centre moved, a circle strait succeeds,
> Another still, and still another spreads;
> Friend, parent, neighbor, first it will embrace;
> His country next; and next all human race.

✦ What role might unlimited love play in why you were created and in your personal journey toward purpose?

PART III

CONSCIOUSLY DIRECTING

YOUR LIFE

CHAPTER 7

Multiplying Our Blessings and Deepening Our Purpose

An attitude of gratitude creates blessings.

—JOHN MARKS TEMPLETON

ARE WE AT A TIME in human evolution where it could be helpful for humanity if more research was directed toward understanding some of the basic spiritual realities such as prayer, love, worship, thanksgiving, and humility? How might individuals benefit from this knowledge? Could researching these realities offer a source of creative possibilities that might flourish were we to consider humbly our role in the quest to discover more of sublime purposes? How could this research help us learn more about why we are created? What areas of daily living could be enhanced from this type of research?

If we approach life in humility of spirit, with an attitude of loving service, how could our purposes make a difference in our world? Have we considered that helping others to discover their purpose might be part of our purpose? Are there various levels of purpose and sometimes changes in direction of purpose? Purpose can range in scope from a primal fight for survival to the highest level of intellectual and spiritual aspiration and expression. Purpose can also change with regard to the circumstances of life. Is it then worth the effort to explore and attempt to discover ongoing purpose throughout our lives? Should we be enthusiastically interested in welcoming and exploring the most simple or the most complex ideas? Could these ideas help us enlarge our personal and global spiritual vision, better comprehend how tiny and temporary we are and how much we have yet to discover?

What inspirational challenges might enrich our understanding with concepts and perspectives that may lead to new discoveries and creative improvements? Can devout participation in a religious or spiritual life sometimes serve as a strong motivator and inspiration in the formation of beneficial qualities of good character? How can the act of worship serve as an invitation to discover higher spiritual energies? How can worship assist us in learning various lessons of life? Is every thought, feeling, and action actually some kind of prayer? What newly discovered wisdom might be found in researching inspired thoughts from the great thinkers and writers from various cultures and religious perspectives?

THE BLESSINGS OF
PERSONAL SPIRITUAL VALUES

Do we experience a shift of personal values when we lift our vision from worldly accomplishment to spiritual discoveries? If so, how does this shift in focus help propel us toward beneficial accomplishments? What do you think are basic spiritual realities? How high would attributes of praise, gratitude, noble purpose, humility, and thanksgiving, for example, rate on your list of character traits and beneficial qualities? How could trust and openness, sensitivity, creativity, stability, honesty, integrity, worship, and devotion help us discover divine purposes?

Could we then direct our actions for the greater good of humanity?

Many people cherish dreams and goals aligned with their personal desires. However, when we lift our vision to Spirit's guidance, do we feel expanded and more deeply connected to higher purposes? Certainly, our lives often seem to take on deeper meaning as we invite the energies of unlimited love, compassion, and radiant spiritual light to be guiding forces in our daily activities. Dr. Viktor Frankl affirms Nietzsche's words, "He who has a why to live for can bear with almost any how."[1] The point is that purpose and meaning can be experienced in many aspects of life.

What steps can we take to explore avenues for creative purpose? What are we willing to do in the present moment? Is a clear process available that could help build a bridge of greater understanding between the visible and invisible realms, the physical and spiritual planes?

FOOD FOR BODY, MIND, AND SPIRIT

Would you think of going without eating regular meals for a week? For two weeks? For three weeks? Probably not! The human body needs life-nourishing food on a regular basis to remain healthy. Without the various nutrients provided by food, the vital energy to keep our muscles firm and strong and our ability to stay active could deteriorate. Our mental processes would slow. Without food, symptoms of malnutrition might soon become evident and we would likely lose the ability to function effectively. Would we foolishly ignore our symptoms, or would we take immediate steps to remedy the situation?

Every living organism needs food for sustenance. Even simple vegetable cells need nourishment. Guided by innate intelligence, the plant absorbs the food that is essential to its growth and development. When grown in a soil and climate that is conducive to growth, the plant flourishes. If grown in soil and climate conditions that are impoverished and devitalized, a corresponding degenerative plant specimen may result.

As we need food on a regular basis to sustain our body's energy, is it not also logical that our soul needs nourishment on a regular basis to maintain spiritual health? What happens when we go without regular spiritual nourishment? (And a quick, occasional "snack" does not get the job done!) We could become mentally, physically, and emotionally unstable. We may feel fearful or inadequate or depleted. We may feel isolated and alone. We might lose our optimistic attitude and become easily upset, angry, or judgmental. We may become sharp and abrasive to others. Relationships may crumble. Our personalities may lose their sparkle. And what happens to our feelings of unlimited love, noble purpose, and high vision? Without spiritual nourishment, are we more likely to become sidetracked from our purposes? Many religions and spiritual traditions refer to a vibratory energy at the core of our being as the divine spark, a higher power, the Spirit, the soul essence, the seat of the sacred, or Spirit's essence. How important is it to reconnect on a regular basis with the inner Spirit to build up reserves of love, wisdom, and self-mastery that far surpass our human resources?

Divine energy is a boundless source of spiritual sustenance, eternally ready and infinitely available. We may feast from the table of spiritual bounty at any time. And what could be more "delicious" and soul satisfying than the spiritual qualities that multiply our blessings, help us discover our purpose in life, and lead us to understanding why we are created?

THE BENEFITS OF PRAISE, GRATITUDE, AND THANKSGIVING

Praise implies an expression of approval, esteem, or commendation. We praise a superb performance. We acknowledge a job well done with sincere words of approval and encouragement. We sing praises to the glory of God. "Praise God from whom all blessings flow!" Praise can help us eliminate stress from our lives by directing our thoughts and mind to be more in tune with the Infinite.

From where do many of the stresses and conflicts in our world arise? Could some of the problems experienced in human life be a result of ignorance? When people seem ignorant of spiritual realities and life purposes, can their values become confused, resulting in inappropriate choices and actions? Could the focus of individual thoughts and feelings be part of the problem? What results might be experienced if, in a stressful situation, conflictive thoughts were halted and replaced with the simple statement: "Praise God for the gift of my life"?

Praising God for life can affirm an attitude of praise and gratitude with the Creator's spirit within. How may resolution of stress, confusion, and inner conflict lead us into increased spiritual growth? How could the words "Praise God for the gift of my life" urge us to reach for higher values or challenge us to explore new areas of discovery? New possibilities often present themselves in the most amazing ways! We may be astounded when we look beyond appearances and uncover the precious treasure of a person or an experience.

Gratitude and thanksgiving are spiritual tools, similar to praise, for transforming many of the stresses and challenges of modern life. Both gratitude and thanksgiving express grateful acknowledgment and feelings of thankful appreciation for benefits received. These spiritual attributes often open the door to increased growth, because they embrace the purpose of creation within itself. True thanksgiving has been described as the soul's recognition of its relation to the Creator. When this recognition occurs, could there be any limit to the soul's capacity for beneficial and fruitful accomplishment?

ACKNOWLEDGING FIVE DAILY BLESSINGS!

When you awaken in the morning, can you think of five things for which you are overwhelmingly grateful? The gift of awakening to a new day could certainly top the list! Try thinking of five blessings as an experiment and notice if your relationships with others improve, if your day flows more harmoniously and happily, and if your life seems more fruitful and successful.

Could one of the major lessons in life be to turn ourselves inside out —and possibly to discover that the purposes we are searching for already exist within us? How do praise, gratitude, and thanksgiving help us live more from the inside out? If we live any day of our lives without giving thanks for the blessings we may claim, are we fully effective? Counting blessings attracts more blessings. Beginning each day by recognizing and acknowledging our blessings extends a rich invitation for increasing blessings.

The rewards of developing a spiritual consciousness of praise, gratitude, and thanksgiving are limitless. Every area of a person's life may be beneficially affected by applying these spiritual attributes in daily living. If the inner light shines brightly, shadows fly from the world, multiplying our blessings and deepening our purposes!

THE HAPPINESS OPTION

Who are the happiest people you know? If you were to write down the names of ten persons who bubble over with happiness, would you find that they radiate love and respect for everyone around them? Could part of their happiness stem from the fact that they may be dedicated to growing spiritually?

Studying happy people can be one way to learn more about happiness. What is the source of their joy? How do they respond to and interact with others? Are they courteous listeners? Do they have a consistently positive attitude? Is there a correlation between their happiness and their character traits? What are their strengths? What are their goals? How do they establish their priorities? Do they find time for research and communion with the inner Spirit? What lessons can we learn from these joyous, wonderful people?

The pursuit of happiness for itself is seldom successful because happiness is a byproduct. If we pursue happiness for personal reasons, it eludes us. If we strive to bring happiness to others, we cannot stop its return to ourselves. The more we seek to give happiness away, the more it returns to us, multiplied and bringing rich blessings and greater clarity to our purposes. When we inspire others to be happy, we inspire ourselves. The world-famous physician and philosopher, Dr. Albert Schweitzer, said, "I don't know what your destiny will be, but one thing I know: the only ones among you who will be really happy are those who will have sought and found how to serve." Deep, abiding happiness derives from spiritual wealth, not from material wealth, and it comes from giving rather than getting.

Abraham Lincoln said, "Most folks are about as happy as they make up their minds to be." This statement seems to indicate that we have a choice, an option. If we each choose our own state of mind and if we ourselves are the belief makers, then can our happiness, along with the beliefs and visions that support it, lay a foundation for an ultimate attitudinal advantage? For example, does making a decision to live a happier life through expressing unlimited love and serving others acknowledge a capacity and ability to choose a spiritual path? Do we then take a directorial role in guiding our responses to people and events?

PERSONAL HAPPINESS

What does happiness mean to us, individually? The feeling or sensation of happiness might be unique to each of us. Intents and purposes in life seem to represent primary distinguishing characteristics for most humans. Living a life filled with direction and purpose can be monumentally important to our happiness. What are some things we can do and ways we can live to achieve a life filled with increasing meaning and purpose?

Gratitude is a personality characteristic that often seems to be displayed when people are happy. When we are happy, we often feel grateful. And when we are grateful, we often are happier. The doorway to increased happiness opens easily. We can share our love, attention, assistance, caring, and support with friends, loved ones, coworkers, children, parents, neighbors, acquaintances—the list could go on and on!

In *Happiness Is a Serious Problem*, Dennis Prager describes six values that are widely held to be more important than happiness—and therefore bring people much happiness as a byproduct! These values are: 1) passionate and meaningful pursuits that give life meaning,

2) becoming a person of greater depth, 3) wisdom defined as understanding rather than knowing, 4) greater clarity in understanding yourself and life, 5) goodness—doing good and attaining good character, and 6) pursuit of the transcendent.[2]

Each of these values can help us cultivate a richer philosophy of life and enable us to take further strides toward discovering and expressing our purposes. If we value growth, would we also likely value the opportunities of every situation that life brings to our experience? Certainly, those who choose to find the positive that can be found in each situation reap the blessings.

INVESTING IN YOURSELF AND INVESTING YOURSELF

Have you heard the maxim, "Anything worth doing at all is worth doing well"? Are these words indicating that when we expend energy in any activity, we are actually investing a vital part of who and what we are into the experience? When deciding upon a career path, how helpful would it be to first research some questions? For instance, what are my natural talents, gifts, and abilities? What stimulates my creativity and enthusiasm? What endeavors stir excitement and a desire for further discovery in me? What needs to be done that I have the ability to accomplish? How can I contribute?

When the work we choose stems from awareness of our gifts, talents, and abilities, and our enthusiasm stimulates an exciting and abundant flow of energy, are we more likely to be "on target" toward achieving our goals and purposes? Would the way we accomplish our jobs change if we perceived our work as developing from the inside out or considered our work representative of our own unique and creative souls? Is the vocation we choose an expression of Spirit working in the world through us? Our work is about much more than being paid to do a job. With deep spirituality, can any work be expressed as a level of service?

In *The Re-Invention of Work: A New Vision of Livelihood for Our Time*, Matthew Fox wrote, "Spirit means life, and both life and livelihood are about living in depth, living with meaning, purpose, joy, and a sense of contributing to the greater community. A spirituality of work is about bringing life and livelihood back together again. And Spirit with them."[3]

Harlow Herbert Curtice, an automobile manufacturer, gave this advice, "Do your job better each time. Do it better than anyone else can do it. Do it better than it needs to be done. Let no one or anything stand between you and the difficult task. I know this sounds old-fashioned. It is, but it has built the world."[4] Doesn't this sound like an excellent recommendation, especially when applied to spiritual growth and purposes? And if we apply this kind of commitment to our spiritual growth, would the beneficial results necessarily overflow into every other area of our lives?

A DEEPER MEANING OF WORK

Hildegard of Bingen once wrote a letter in which she stated that she wanted above all else to be "useful." And the *Bhagavad Gita* tells us, "Who in all one's work sees God, that one in truth goes unto God: God is that person's worship. God is that one's offering, offered by God in the fire of God."[5] Could we become more "useful" by considering and exploring the idea of our work as a possible fertile field for progress of the human species?

Investing ourselves in our work can reflect a joyous elixir of life. Do you experience joy in your work? Do the results of your work bring joy to others? How does your work contribute to the ongoing great work of the universe? How creative is your work?

Imagine a new building that is under construction. The foundation is poured and set. The structure and framework rises daily, step-by-step. Eventually the roof is installed. At the proper time, the plumbers, the electricians, the floor-covering workers, and the painters arrive on the scene to accomplish their tasks. Eventually, the landscapers add the finishing touches.

How can this building represent our lives? What type of design and form of construction have we chosen for building our lives? How do we prepare and plan to begin the work? Do we dig deep into the earth and pour a strong and lasting foundation? Do we build our lives step-by-step, with regularity and perseverance? Do we refrain from any tendency to skip a step in the building process or allow ourselves to become stuck in a particular area? Do we select quality materials by grounding our energies in spiritual principles? Do we enrich our minds and emotions regularly with prayer?

We may not be able to control or stop some of the changing situations and circumstances in our lives, but what are some ways we can develop focus, poise, and discernment as skills in developing our spiritual lives? Modest goals may require a few steps in a simple process. Larger and more far-reaching goals may require a longer and more demanding process. In either case, when we invest in ourselves by choosing the high road of spiritual growth, can we then competently and successfully invest ourselves in whatever work we may choose as beneficial? Joyfully, our individual purposes can continue to evolve throughout our lifetimes as we catch glimpses of the bigger picture of life.

LIVING AND WORKING PURPOSEFULLY

Who or what causes apple trees to blossom in the spring? Who or what causes the tiny embryo to develop into a human being? Who or what causes our hearts to beat and our bodies to function in rhythmic harmony? What are the unseen forces that hold the planets in their orbits and sprinkle the galaxies with stardust? Who or what prompts the inner voice that continues to encourage us that there may be more to life than we may presently be experiencing?

When we learn how to discover and connect with creative realities, have we taken a major step toward living and working with spiritual purposes? As we utilize the knowledge we glean through spiritual disciplines and techniques and an understanding of working with spiritual principles and universal laws, we advance on our way toward finding spiritual solutions to most problems.

Perhaps in recognizing that we are more than our minds, that we can find our way out of psychological pain, and that we can experience joy and embrace our better selves in the present moment, we begin to open ourselves to the transforming experience of creativity.

Does clarifying our individual purposes help satisfy the basic human need to realize that we are created for a reason? How does being in touch with our own "calling" promote a more authentic expression of our real selves? How does a realization of purpose help us make sense of the meaning of life? A roadmap of purpose is rarely handed to us, complete with instructions! It usually comes because we choose to learn more about ourselves and about why we are here. We may be capable of reaching a state of conscious awareness that we never imagined!

Someone once recommended, "Let life question you." Are you open to being questioned by life in order to discover more of who you are, why you were created, and what is your purpose?

Reflections on Life

In *The Eye of the I*, Dr. David Hawkins wrote:

> The spiritual pathway is facilitated by certain characteristics which become reinforced and more powerful with practice, experience, and success. These include the capacity to focus unswervingly on a goal and to concentrate fixedly on a technique or spiritual exercise with commitment and dedication. Thus, there is a resolution of purpose and a willingness to let go of everything or anything based upon one's profound belief and faith in spiritual teaching or truth. In general, there is a willingness to forgive and love rather than to hate and condemn. There is a willingness to forsake the lesser for the greater and a desire to understand rather than to judge. . . . Perhaps the most useful tool is the capacity for humility and the realization of the limitations of ordinary consciousness and their consequences.[6]

Part of fulfilling our purposes may involve learning how to accept difficulty with graciousness, growing through our mistakes, and reorienting ourselves when we may feel we have lost our way. How does searching daily for ways to improve enable us to multiply our blessings and deepen our purpose?

CHAPTER 8

Discoveries!

Life is filled with infinite possibilities.
—JOHN MARKS TEMPLETON

The Harvard biologist Edward O. Wilson wrote,

> The search for spirituality is going to be one of the major his-
> torical episodes of the 21st century. We realize that we are going
> to have to be proactive in seeking it and defining it instead of
> reactive in the traditional manner of taking the sacred texts and
> beliefs handed down to us and trying to adapt them to an evolv-
> ing culture. That's just not working any more. We need to create
> a new epic based on the origins of humanity.[1]

UNLIMITED SEARCH and discovery about spiritual realities
could be an exciting challenge and a tremendous opportunity! What research using scientific methods to explore
spiritual realities has already begun?

Science has achieved amazing success in understanding details of the
world around us. What further attitudes and endeavors can guide us
toward additional, accelerating discoveries? What glimmers of knowing may be discovered within the horizons of the limitless unknown?
What evidences of creative accelerating discoveries are provided by

the visible universe? How may we research and discover possibilities of the invisible universe? Are the laws of infinity the same or different from the laws of the finite? Or do universal laws apply to both? Does the progress of science and theology show that humans are endowed with creative and perceptive capacities that are helpful in the pursuit of truth? Why is it vital to search for humanity's purpose? Are we, as humans, all part of the same universal divinity? Are we any more or any less significant than anything else in the universe? What is the purpose for humans and for human purposes?

Johann Wolfgang von Goethe said, "The universe is a harmonious whole, each creature but a note, a shade of great harmony, which man must study in its entirety and greatness, lest each detail should remain a dead letter." We may today know far more than preceding generations, yet do we understand even one percent of what can be discovered? The more answers we get to our questions about the universe and man's function in the universe, the more questions arise.

How does enthusiasm for seeking new information and improving older concepts open wider avenues for research and discovery? How many of our concepts of God need to be enlarged in the light of what we have presently discovered about the universe? Increasingly, we are finding ways to expand our perceptive abilities. Life seems to be filled with infinite possibilities. What are the lessons of life? What can be learned from what we have recently discovered of life's origin on our planet? Its nature? Its unity? Its history? How common is life in the cosmos, and how long will our species survive? Mysteriously, we seem to be able to participate in, and even accelerate, creativity. Is it possible that humans were created as agents for that purpose? Whatever the response, we humans continue to engage in an ongoing quest for discovery of spiritual realities. We seek purpose and meaning by researching the varied evidences presented by life to each of us.

BEING WHO WE ARE

Do humans experience accelerated growth through increased self-awareness, self-analysis, self-improvement, and self-acceptance? Self-awareness means we can face who, what, and where we are in life with complete honesty and be in integrity with what we learn. Could recognizing, accepting, and expressing our authentic spiritual reality represent part of a foundation for personal honesty, discovery, and purpose?

When we attempt this personal overview, an array of thoughts, feelings, emotions, and experiences may parade before our consciousness. Our growing awareness can provide deeply meaningful insights and understanding. How can we reconcile our personal ideals with practical everyday reality? Do our ideals reflect our highest vision of possibilities for ourselves and for the world? What is your vision? Does your vision and purpose inspire you and fill you with hope, enthusiasm, anticipation, and direction?

How important is it to stay apprised of the inner world of spirit? Are we able to see divine blessings everywhere, in everyone, and in every situation? How do we build our lives on a foundation of spiritual principles? Are we receptive to learning new ways to focus on clear goals and follow step-by-step plans or guidelines toward our destiny and purposes? What is the meaning of "As we live according to our highest light, more light will be given"?

The story of Mahatma Gandhi is one of a once nervous, neurotic, and fearful man, who learned to look within his innermost being and gradually, relentlessly, freed himself from his limitations. And millions of others traveled the road to freedom with him! Gandhi refused to compromise his integrity, regardless of circumstances. Although he was scorned at first and his life seemed difficult, the world later beat a path to his door. It is truly beneficial to comprehend that there is a spiritual solution and response to every problem, question, situation, circumstance, and opportunity!

The Bible tells us we are "made in the image and likeness of God." What does this mean? How would we describe our perception of the image and likeness of the Creator? Could this mean the divine presence resides as the deepest and most intimate spiritual reality within each human personality? Could this inner-spirit spark radiate the Creator's unlimited love and creativity directly through each one of us? Can the sacred presence provide a source of spiritual guidance?

Arthur Peacocke wrote in a recent issue of *Research News*:

We can see science and the arts as being aspects of human creativity and that God intended humans to be creative and so share in the divine creativity, as humanity was conceived to be in the image of God. God wants us to be creative individuals in our own spheres, whether it is kicking a ball, writing a poem, discovering a new comet, or whatever.[2]

Yes! The creative energy of divine Spirit can be channeled into any form of expression such as fine arts, crafts, healing, business, science, gardening, design, construction, caring for a family, and so much more.

How can we each develop a greater sense of inner confidence that allows us to manifest our creativity more fully? What activities may be encouraged toward finding our purpose when we shift our perception to cultivate noble goals as part of our vision? What is a workable spiritual approach for individual self-inquiry?

TRUSTING THE SPIRITUAL PROCESS

Have you ever admired someone who seemed to be willing to trust the process of living as they experienced the unfolding of day-to-day activities? Such a person often makes an exciting and creative adventure out of this journey of life. Often, he or she proceeds with confidence, enthusiasm, and joy, is usually successful in most endeavors, and exudes an aura of energetic vitality.

Closer association with persons of this nature may indicate that they, too, made mistakes along the way. However, they learned equally from their successes and their errors. Possibly some of these experiences may have opened a doorway for discovery into realms of the Spirit. Sometimes something seemingly miraculous happened! They may have learned of a larger process of living — a spiritual process — that changed how they respond to the world around them. Norvin McGranahan said, "When a man begins to understand himself he begins to live. When he begins to live, he begins to understand his fellow men."

Utilizing spiritual tools in daily living can provide a beneficial system for finding, developing, and living out our purposes. Laws of Life and universal principles represent noble patterns of spiritual expression to which human behavior may aspire. The Laws of Life represent universal principles of the invisible world that can be described and tested by extensive and rigorous examination of human behavior. These laws operate without bias or prejudice and work for the highest good of all. They provide effective spiritual roadmaps upon which we can rely because they are constant. The bottom line is that they work! These principles provide a process of spiritual growth and discovery that remains trustworthy and dependable! It is left to each individual to decide to learn more about these precious tools and about ways to live life in accordance with their guidance.

RECOGNIZING THE PRESENCE OF THE SACRED

What is the importance of recognizing the presence of the sacred within us and around us? Perhaps an effective starting point for our spiritual research would be a realization that the universe, and our participation in it, seems to be much more than a haphazard occurrence. Infinite invisible intelligence is reflected by everything in the universe. At least, this seems to be the understanding from the perspective of finite creatures in a vast universe of infinite complexity and intricacy! Much evidence for deep meaning seems to be written into the laws and processes of nature. The extraordinary complexity of life invites discussion about the marvelous creativity and connection of all living things. The process of creation seems to seethe with innovations and a superb timing that reduce the possibility of blind chance. Could any activity be more relevant to our inner lives than to research the presence of the sacred in everyone and every thing? To regard with respect or reverence the divinity of the great mysteries that seem to be present everywhere?

Ancient spiritual writings suggest that our purpose on Earth may be to emerge from lower levels of living to higher planes of evolving consciousness. Does this idea mean that possibly every experience provided by life can serve as an opportunity to grow? Is part of evolution through discovery a realization that everything is a part of the Creator?

HOW MAY PRAYER HELP US FIND GREATER PURPOSE?

Prayer is an effective avenue for touching and communing with divine Spirit energy and experiencing what some may call "the attributes of God." A personal, cultural, or spiritual approach to prayer often relates to an individual's concept of the Creator and the universal creative process. Regardless of where our life paths may lead us or what we may choose to do in life, a consciousness of prayer can help us do better. As we become aware of this uplifting in consciousness, we may ask to become a conduit through which the Creator's love and wisdom may flow. Can we guide our actions to be in harmony with God's purposes for us?

In his classic book, *The Varieties of Religious Experience,* William James defined prayer as "every kind of inward communion or conversation with the power recognized as divine." Other scholars have suggested that this communion is often expressed in two primary forms: verbal prayer and meditative prayer—speaking to God and listening to God. Some surveys (by Gallup, for example) indicate that the closer people feel to the Creative source, the better they may feel about themselves. Whatever the form, a vast number of people regularly engage in prayer. And prayer often generates what has been described as a more mature and healthy form of spirituality.

PERSONAL PRAYER PERSPECTIVES

Does prayer change us? If so, how? Through what process? Does prayer make a difference in our lives? Does a prayer life bring us closer to the Creator? Do our prayers change the way we relate to others and help us develop more loving relationships? Do our prayers help us deal with our personal sense of self-worth? Is personal transformation one measurable result of prayer? How does prayer help us transform the old self into a new self? Can prayer be a personal wellspring for a productive life? What is the divine/human interaction through prayer and inspiration and through participation in some beneficial action?

What do people do when they pray? Søren Kierkegaard wrote in his 1846 *Journal*:

> The immediate person thinks and imagines that when he prays, the important thing, the thing he must concentrate upon, is that *God should hear what he is praying for*. And yet in the true, eternal sense, it is just the reverse; the true relation in prayer is not only when God hears what is prayed for, but when *the person praying continues to pray until he is* the one who hears, who hears what God wills. The immediate person, therefore, uses many words and . . . makes demands in his prayer. The true man of prayer only *attends*.[3]

Does God really speak to individuals? And are we listening? Scriptures tell us that the Creator promises to reveal himself to those who seek: "For God speaks in one way and in two, although man does not perceive it" (Job 33:14). Evidences noted from the most fundamental religious or transcendent experiences seem to indicate that these "peak" experiences, often resulting from prayer, may indeed be more commonplace than we realize. These encounters are often regarded as interpersonal experiences that involve a sense of intimacy between the person who prays and the creative Source. The person in prayer may sense or feel the existence or presence of divine energy. Some have indicated that the practice of prayer is a place of spiritual communion much deeper and more delicate to the soul than mere words can describe.

How can prayer experiences make a difference in a person's life? From one perspective, could a prayerful consciousness be considered an aspect of creative thinking in the maturation and progress of the soul? Does prayer put us in touch with the creative truth within ourselves? Is there a relatively strong relationship between experiencing divine energy in prayer and a closer intimacy with the Creator? Prayer provides many blessings and the effects from regular prayer may often be profound. A person may find greater purpose and meaning in life, increased satisfaction in day-to-day-living, guidance and inspiration for decision making, the ability to forgive others, and deeper insights into spiritual truths and principles. Prayer can provide an element of acknowledgment and acceptance of the experiences in life in a powerful and transformational way.

BUILDING SPIRITUAL HABITS

The ethics of our habits, personality expressions, and character can often make us or break us! We may be our own best friends or our own worst enemies! A lot of helpful truth can be found in these words. When we have a tendency to perform or behave in a certain way, a defined pattern of living begins to emerge. Spiritual principles of effective living can help us achieve the success, happiness, and progress we desire. Therefore, would it not be totally beneficial for each of us to live life and behave in ways that build spiritual habits?

In this book, we have written of spiritual principles, universal laws of life, divine purpose, learning more about why we are here, understanding more of who and what we are as part of divine creation, and finding our individual life purposes. We considered the importance of consciously integrating the many unifying forces of Spirit into our daily living. We acknowledged the possibility that our soul may grow through the combined efforts of the human mind and the inner Spirit. We contemplated how our minds provide a constant flow of raw materials and how the Spirit winnows intrinsic spiritual worth from these experiences. Thus, universal Spirit initiates and nurtures our souls.

When our thoughts shift to the realm of Spirit, the physical and emotional realms often spontaneously respond to the higher call. When choosing to work in harmony with spiritual principles, we may notice how various aspects of our lives begin to improve. The spiritually wise person learns to distinguish between constructive and destructive behaviors and habits. A shift to new and refined behaviors often brings increased synchronization between mind, body, and spirit. And, oh, the rich, abundant blessings that can unfold!

Then, with the realization and consideration that as residents of planet Earth we may be on a sacred quest, we can strengthen our desire to discover and choose the spiritual path. We begin to deny the demands of the limited human ego and acknowledge our higher spiritual nature. We may be urged onward by the loving, sacred presence within us to perhaps make a shift in consciousness, find our individual purpose, and tap into the unified field of all possibilities of the universe within us. As we follow the invitation to explore our sacred quest, we can work individually and collectively on noble goals and continue to find accelerating levels of opportunities for expression and contribution to greater good.

The Power to Choose

Perhaps a primary quality of the spiritual life could be that of maintaining an attitude where we look at life not as a place to accumulate wealth or gain great power or placate egotistical personal desires, but as an opportunity for research, exploration, discovery, and learning. And we can learn from even the smallest details of life. Choosing a spiritual attitude regarding life can lead us to be more loving, productive, friendly, and benevolent toward every person or situation we encounter throughout our day. Our lives are filtered through our own perceptions. "What is going on" consists primarily of our attitudes and perceptions toward situations rather than self-existent, external realities. It appears we have been given everything we need to evolve. Part of our task may be to discover and use our opportunities in an enthusiastic, appropriate, and helpful manner.

Richard J. Leider wrote in *The Power of Purpose*:

Knowing who we are, why we are here, and what we're trying to do with our lives enriches our journey. Whether our purpose is to serve God, to raise healthy children, to create a healthier environment, or to play beautiful music, we are empowered by the purpose.

We may not always see the results our work has on others, but we know deep down that there is some contribution, large or small, to the bigger picture. We know that we made a difference, that our life mattered.[4]

DISCOVERING NEW FRONTIERS

A major focus of the new century may be fostering an expanded vision of God that is informed by recent discoveries of science about the nature of the universe and the place of humans in God's universe. The stage is set for keen and creative minds to launch out on a new exploration of theology, respectful of our great religious heritage but focusing on new possibilities of the twenty-first century. Can we have a more comprehensive, more exploratory, more humble theology? How might we go about exploring the possibly rich texture of the unseen?

If each branch of science is showing that creation is vastly wider and more complex than comprehended two millennia ago—or even just one century ago—does this reveal a more worshipful Creator? Is trying to help in God's creative processes a way to express our worship and thankfulness? We learn that in a vast and intricate cosmos, there is still much more to be discovered.

When seeking to learn more of who we are and why we were created, would it be pertinent to ask some soul-searching questions? How large is our God? Is he only a wise father? Is he the god of a single race or tribe or planet? Is he somehow separate from reality, or is he the only reality? Besides searching for forms of intelligence in the vast cosmos, should we search for intelligence around us and within us but not yet comprehensible by us?

REFLECTIONS ON LIFE

South African Nobel Peace Prize winner and Anglican Archbishop Desmond Tutu wrote the following reflection on why we were created.

The evolution of the world is a great manifestation of God. As scientists understand more and more about the interdependence not only of living things but of rocks, rivers — the whole of the universe — I am left in awe that I, too, am a part of this tremendous miracle. Not only am I a part of this pulsating network, but I am an indispensable part. It is not only theology that teaches me this, but it is the truth that environmentalists shout from the rooftops. Every living creature is an essential part of the whole.

All creatures have special attributes. Our particular attribute is the ability to reason. With reason we are enabled to react independently from our environment. What are we supposed to do?

Our surroundings are awesome. We see about us majestic mountains, the perfection of a tiny mouse, a newborn baby, a flower, the colors of a seashell. Each creature is most fully that which it is created to be, an almost incredible reflection of the infinite, the invisible, the indefinable. All women and men participate in that reflected glory.

We believe that we are in fact the image of our Creator. Our response must be to live up to that amazing potential — to give God glory by reflecting His beauty and His love. That is why we are here and that is the purpose of our lives. In that response we enter most fully into relationships with God, our fellow men and women, and we are in harmony with all creation.[5]

Notes

INTRODUCTION

1. John M. Templeton and Robert L. Herrmann, *The God Who Would Be Known* (New York: Harper & Row, 1989), 13.

2. Andrew Wilson, ed. *World Scriptures: A Comparative Anthology of Sacred Texts* (St. Paul, Minn.: Paragon House, 1995), 212.

CHAPTER 1

1. Daniel H. Osmond, "A Physiologist Looks at Purpose and Meaning in Life," in *Evidence of Purpose*, ed. John M. Templeton (New York: Continuum, 1994), 134–35.

2. Walter Starke, *It's All God* (Boerne, Tex.: Guadalupe Press, 1998), 236.

3. John M. Templeton and Robert L. Herrmann, *The God Who Would Be Known* (New York: Harper & Row, 1989), 4–5.

4. Richard J. Leider, *The Power of Purpose* (New York: MJF Books, 1997), 3–4.

5. Ralph Waldo Trine, quoted in John M. Templeton, *Possibilities of Over One Hundredfold More Spiritual Information: The Humble Approach in Science and Theology* (Philadelphia: Templeton Foundation Press, 2000), 135.

CHAPTER 2

1. Owen Gingerich, "Dare a Scientist Believe in Design?" *Evidence of Purpose*, ed. John M. Templeton (New York: Continuum, 1994), 29.

2. Piero Ferrucci, *What We May Be* (Los Angeles: J.P. Tarcher, 1982), 60.

3. Eckhart Tolle, *The Power of Now* (Novato, Calif.: New World Library, 1991), 46.

CHAPTER 3

1. Barbara Brennan, quoted in David Friend and Editors of *Life*, *The Meaning of Life* (Boston: Little, Brown, 1991), 121.

2. Charles T. Tart, *Living the Mindful Life* (Boston: Shamballa, 1991), 27.

3. Freeman Dyson, quoted in Wayne W. Dyer, *Wisdom of the Ages* (New York: Harper Collins, 1998), 134.

4. Paramahansa Yoganananda, *Man's Eternal Quest* (Los Angeles: Self-Realization Fellowship, 1975), 110.

CHAPTER 4

1. Andrew Wilson, ed. *World Scriptures: A Comparative Anthology of Sacred Texts* (St. Paul, Minn.: Paragon House, 1995), 212.

2. Rosa Parks, quoted in David Friend and Editors of *Life*, *The Meaning of Life* (Boston: Little, Brown, 1991), 87.

CHAPTER 5

1. Imelda Shanklin, *What Are You?* (Unity Village, Mo.: Unity Books, 1929), 22.

2. Gregg Braden, *Awakening to Zero Point* (Bellevue, Wash.: Radio Bookstore Press, 1997), 195.

3. Alphonse de Châteaubriant and Marcus Aurelius, quoted in Piero Ferrucci, *What We May Be* (Los Angeles: J.P. Tarcher, 1982), 103.

4. Eckhart Tolle, *The Power of Now* (Novato, Calif.: New World Library, 1991), 9.

5. Ken Wilber, *The Spectrum of Consciousness* (Wheaton, Ill.: Theosophical Publishing House, 1977), 53.

6. Ralph Waldo Trine, *In Tune With the Infinite* (Indianapolis: Bobbs-Merrill, 1957), 169.

7. Frank Tyger, quoted in John M. Templeton, *Worldwide Laws of Life: 200 Eternal Spiritual Principles* (Philadelphia: Templeton Foundation Press, 1997), 27.

CHAPTER 6

1. Wayne Dyer, *Your Sacred Self* (New York: Harper, 1995), 243.

2. Emmanuel Swedenborg, *Divine Love and Wisdom* (New York: Citadel Press, 1963), 2.

3. Pitirim A. Sorokin, *The Ways and Power of Love* (Philadelphia: Templeton Foundation Press, 2002), 11.

4. Emmet Fox, *Power Through Constructive Thinking* (San Francisco: Harper, 1989).

5. Pitirim A. Sorokin, *Ways and Power of Love*, xvii.

6. Teilhard de Chardin, *The Future of Man* (New York: Harper, 1959), 78–79.

7. Timothy Ferris, "The Other Einstein," *Science 83* (October 1982): 25–26.

CHAPTER 7

1. Viktor Frankl, quoted in *Evidence of Purpose*, ed. John M. Templeton (New York: Continuum, 1994), 142.

2. Dennis Prager, *Happiness Is a Serious Problem* (New York: Regan Books/ Harper-Collins, 1998), 107–113.

3. Matthew Fox, *The Re-Invention of Work: A New Vision of Livelihood for Our Time* (New York: Harper-Collins, 1995), 1–2.

4. John M. Templeton with James Ellison, *The Templeton Plan: 21 Steps to Personal Success and Real Happiness* (New York: Harper, 1987), 49.

5. Juan Mascaro, trans., *Bhagavad Gita* (Middlesex, U.K.: Penguin Books, 1962), 63.

6. David Hawkins, *The Eye of the I* (Sedona, Ariz.: Veritas Publishing, 2001), 32.

CHAPTER 8

1. Edward O. Wilson, quoted in Robert L. Herrmann, ed., *Expanding Humanity's Vision of God* (Philadelphia: Templeton Foundation Press, 2001), 294.

2. Arthur Peacocke, *Research News and Opportunities in Science and Theology* (July/August 2002), 6.

3. Margaret M. Poloma and George H. Gallup Jr., *Varieties of Prayer* (Philadelphia: Trinity Press International, 1991), 19.

4. Richard J. Leider, *The Power of Purpose* (New York: MJF Books, 1997), 140.

5. Desmond Tutu, quoted in David Friend and Editors of *Life* Magazine, *The Meaning of Life* (Boston: Little, Brown, 1991), 13.

Selected Bibliography
and Recommended Reading

Abbott, Edward A. *Flatland*. New York: Penguin, 1952.

Dossey, Larry, M.D. *Recovering the Soul*. New York: Bantam, 1989.

Dyer, Wayne, *There's a Spiritual Solution to Every Problem*. New York: HarperCollins, 2001.

Fox, Matthew. *The Reinvention of Work*. San Francisco: HarperCollins, 1995.

Herrmann, Robert L. *Expanding Humanity's Vision of God*. Philadelphia: Templeton Foundation Press, 2001.

Leider, Richard J. *The Power of Purpose*. New York: MJF Books, 1997.

Sorokin, Pritirim A. *The Ways and Power of Love*. Philadelphia: Templeton Foundation Press, 2002.

Starke, Walter. *It's All God*. Boerne, Tex.: Guadalupe Press, 1998.

Tart, Charles T. *Living the Mindful Life*. Boston: Shamballa Publications, 1994.

Templeton, John M. *Worldwide Laws of Life: 200 Eternal Spiritual Principles*. Philadelphia: Templeton Foundation Press, 1997.

_____. *Wisdom from World Religions: Pathways Toward Heaven on Earth*. Philadelphia: Templeton Foundation Press, 2002.

_____. *How Large Is God? The Voices of Scientists and Theologians*. Philadelphia: Templeton Foundation Press ,1997.

_____. *The Humble Approach*. Philadelphia: Templeton Foundation Press, 1995.

_____. *Possibilities for Over One Hundredfold More Spiritual Information*. Philadelphia: Templeton Foundation Press, 2000.

_____. *Evidence of Purpose: Scientists Discover the Creator*. New York: Continuum, 1994.

_____. *Spiritual Evolution: Scientists Discuss Their Beliefs*. Philadelphia: Templeton Foundation Press, 1998.

Templeton, John M. and Robert L. Herrmann. *The God Who Would Be Known: Revelations of the Divine in Contemporary Science*. Philadelphia: Templeton Foundation Press, 1998,

————. *Is God the Only Reality?* New York: Continuum, 1994.

Templeton, John M. and Rebekah Alezander Dunlap. *Story of a Clam: A Fable of Discovery and Enlightenment*. Philadelphia: Templeton Foundation Press, 2001.

Tolle, Eckhart. *The Power of Now*. Novato, Calif.: New World Library, 1999.

Trine, Ralph Waldo. *In Tune with the Infinite*. Indianapolis: Bobbs-Merrill, 1908.

Wilber, Ken. *The Spectrum of Consciousness*. Wheaton, Ill.: Theosophical Publishing House, 1977.